TEACHER'S PET PUBLICATIONS

LITPLAN TEACHER PACK
for
Out of the Dust
based on the book by
Karen Hesse

Written by
Marion B. Hoffman

© 1999 Teacher's Pet Publications
All Rights Reserved

This **LitPlan** on Karen Hesse's
Out of the Dust
has been brought to you by Teacher's Pet Publications, Inc.

Copyright Teacher's Pet Publications 1999

Only the student materials in this unit plan may be reproduced. Pages such as worksheets and study guides may be reproduced for use in the purchaser's classroom. For any additional copyright questions, contact Teacher's Pet Publications.

Table of Contents
Out of the Dust

Introduction	4
A Few Words about the Author	7
Unit Objectives	9
Reading Assignment Sheet	10
Unit Outline	11
Study Questions (Short Answer)	15
Quiz/Study Questions (Multiple Choice)	30
Pre-reading Vocabulary Worksheets	61
Lesson One (Introductory Lesson)	79
Nonfiction Assignment Sheet	81
Oral Reading Evaluation Form	82
Writing Assignment #1	89
Writing Assignment #2	99
Writing Assignment #3	109
Vocabulary Review Activities	116
Extra Writing Assignments/Discussion ?s	111
Unit Review Activities	118
Unit Tests	121
Unit Resource Materials	147
Vocabulary Resource Materials	163

Introduction
Out of the Dust

This unit plan has been carefully designed to give teachers all of the tools they need to present twenty-four daily lessons on Karen Hesse's novel, **Out of the Dust**. All exercises, activities, and assignments in the unit will develop students' reading, writing, thinking, and language skills. In addition to the essential elements, the unit contains a wide variety of extra resource materials and suggested activities.

The **first lesson** uses a bulletin board activity to introduce the theme of having a dream. All subsequent lessons are designed to maximize the teacher's time while assuring that students at a variety of learning levels are able to progress successfully through the novel.

Reading assignments consist of chronological clusters of poems. The clusters are called sections. The assignments average fifteen pages in length, but that number is deceiving because the poems are often filled with information and dense with emotion and meaning. Students do approximately 15 minutes of pre-reading work in conjunction with each reading assignment. Pre-reading involves reviewing the study questions for the assignment and doing some brief vocabulary work connected to the section of reading.

The **study guide questions** are fact based; the answers are right in the text. These questions come in two formats: short answer or multiple choice. It is probably best to use the short answer questions as study guides for students and the multiple choice version for occasional quizzes.

The **vocabulary work** is intended to enrich students' vocabularies and to aid in their understanding of the book. Students will complete a two-part vocabulary worksheet for each section of reading. Part I focuses on students' use of general knowledge and contextual clues by giving the sentence in which the word appears in the text. Students then write down what they think the words mean based on their usage. Part II nails down the definitions of the words by giving students dictionary definitions of the words and asking students to match the words to the correct definitions.

Although students can attempt the vocabulary work prior to reading the appropriate section of the book, it is probably best to encourage students to do the vocabulary work while they are reading. Thus the contextual clues that students use in understanding the words would include not just those in the individual quotes but those in sentences surrounding the quote and often in the entire poem. By the time that students have finished the reading assignment and completed the companion worksheet, they should have a clear understanding of the meaning of each word.

Students should be encouraged to use the study guide questions to round out their understanding of the text and to prepare for the unit test. The material covered in these questions serves as a way of reviewing the most important events and ideas presented in the reading assignments.

Dust Introduction continued page 2

In this unit there is a **Critical Based Questions Option**, which gives the teacher a choice of adding to the fact-based questions some questions that require more critical thought. These will be found in Lessons Eight, Nine, Eleven, Thirteen, Fourteen, Fifteen, and Seventeen. Teachers may use all, some, or none of these optional questions.

There are there **writing assignments** in this unit.

The first assignment, in Lesson Five, asks students to write from personal experience. They may write about their own lives, mirroring the kinds of information conveyed by Billie Jo Kelby in the novel, or they may write about Billie Jo herself, explaining why they would or would not like to have Billie Jo as their close friend. Either choice will encourage students to examine the text closely and to try to understand the heroine better.

The second writing assignment, in Lesson Ten, asks that students write to inform. Here students have an opportunity to choose something that they do well and then to explain to an audience how to do the activity. Because not all students know how to do something that they consider to be particularly interesting, they are encouraged to look even at activities like getting from one location to another, traveling the route they take to school. The activity doesn't matter so much as that the students have an opportunity to examine a procedure, looking closely at its parts and explaining how to do the activity to another person.

The third writing assignment, found in Lesson Eighteen, requires students to write to persuade. Because they should have a firm grasp of the novel at this point in the unit, students are asked to write persuasively about it. The assignment requires the students to exercise judgment, to set criteria for what is good and what is bad in their opinion, and then to argue that **Out of the Dust** is either a good or a bad book.

The **nonfiction reading assignment** in this unit focuses on modern farming and is a precursor to the major class project topic. For the nonfiction assignment, students are given a variety of topics relative to modern farming and asked to choose one and read about it. After reading their nonfiction pieces, students will fill out a worksheet on which they answer questions regarding facts, interpretation, criticism, and personal opinions. You are also provided with a KWL (What I Know, What I Want To Know, What I Learned) Sheet that may facilitate students' nonfiction reading.

The major **class project** is optional. Project Modern Farming is an attempt to get students to move beyond the knowledge they acquire through reading the novel to gain firsthand understanding of the situation faced by farmers in America today. The project is geared to having students discover concerns that need addressing and then to address those concerns in meaningful ways.

Dust Introduction continued page 3

You are encouraged to do **group activities** whenever time and circumstances permit. Numerous opportunities are possible for group activities throughout the unit.

Students also will have ample opportunity for **reading aloud** and **making presentations.** Also, a great deal of opportunity will present itself for having rich class discussions about the novel and relevant ancillary topics.

One of the most flexible sections of the unit is the **Extra Discussion Questions/Writing Assignments.** In this section you will find interpretive, critical, critical/personal, and personal response questions and quotations from the text that can be used in a number of ways. Some of these questions and quotations are used as the basis for parts of the unit tests.

Review lessons offer chances to review the novel's main events and ideas and to re-examine its characters through **vocabulary review** and **review with games and puzzles**.

The **unit test** comes in five different formats: two different Short Answer Unit Tests, one Advanced Short Answer Unit Test, and two different Multiple Choice Unit Tests. Answer keys are given for all parts of all tests except for the subjective questions that appear in some of the tests.

There are additional **support materials** included with this unit. The **extra activities packet** includes suggestions for an in-class library, crossword and word search puzzles related to the novel, and extra vocabulary worksheets. There is a list of **bulletin board ideas** which gives the teacher suggestions for a variety of bulletin boards to supplement the unit. In addition, there is a section called **More Activities** which provides the teacher with even more valuable activities to choose from.

Student materials throughout the unit may be reproduced for use in the teacher's classroom without infringement of copyrights. For a fuller statement of the Teacher's Pet Publications copyright policy, see the back of the title page in this unit.

A Few Words About the Author and Her Work

It is not usual in a Teacher's Pet LitPlan for the writer of the plan to plug the book about which it is written. And this is not really a plug, but an explanation. Despite having captured the coveted Newbery Medal for 1998 and being a marvelously interesting book, **Out of the Dust** is a novel that might take a little selling to young readers. For the book is written in free-verse poems.

Let me explain a little further. While I was writing this unit plan, I made a point of mentioning **Out of the Dust** to one of our local librarians. Noticing her with children visiting the library that evening, I could see that she had a special rapport with young readers. So I told her that if she was in the habit of recommending good books to young readers, this would be an excellent choice to recommend. I went so far as to say that the fourteen-year-old protagonist will be liked by readers of all ages. The librarian listened politely, smiled, and then, with a kind of sigh, said, "It's so hard to get children to read poetry."

Because I myself had wondered about the advisability of Karen Hesse's having written the whole book in blank verse form, I was ready with my response. First, the poems are not the rhyming kind that might turn so many children off. They are in blank verse and their voice is very compelling and sure to reach young readers. I even went so far as to say that the poems are "not really poems." I offered the book, open, back to the librarian for her to take a look at one of the "poems." Oh, they're like little journal entries," she said, with new understanding.

And I think she has put her finger on it. The whole novel is filled with little journal entries that allow Billie Jo Kelby, the heroine of the book, to speak in an unaffected, authentic fourteen-year-old voice. One short entry will suffice. Billie Jo and her classmates are regularly given achievement tests at their school:

> *While we sat*
> *taking our six-weeks test,*
> *the wind rose*
> *and the sand blew*
> *right through the cracks in the schoolhouse wall,*
> *right through the gaps around the window glass,*
> *and by the time the tests were done,*
> *each and every one of us*
> *was coughing pretty good and we all*
> *needed a bath.*
> *I hope we get bonus points*
> *for testing in a dust storm.*

April 1934

Dust A Few Words continued page 2

None of the poems is hard to read. None contains very difficult language. None is longer than four printed pages. Each adds something interesting to the reader's understanding of Billie Jo Kelby, her family, friends, and neighbors, and their lives in Oklahoma in 1934 and 1935.

I tell you all of this as fair warning. If you really want your students to like this book, you might take a few minutes before the first lesson to "sell" the book. Maybe you even want to talk about journal entries and let your students discover the word "poems" later on their own. The rewriting exercise in the third lesson of the plan might further help to dispel the notion that young readers are actually reading indulging in poetry.

The novel was, of course, written by Karen Hesse, who has written a number of other works. She is the author of **The Music of Dolphins**, **A Time of Angels**, **Phoenix Rising**, **Letters from Rifka**, and **Wish on a Unicorn.** For even younger readers, she has written **Lavender**, **Sable**, **Poppy's Chair**, and **Lester's Dog**.

Out of the Dust is a *Publisher's Weekly* Best Book of the Year, A *School Library Journal* Best Book of the Year, A *Booklist* Editors' Choice, A *Booklinks* Best Book of the Year, and is a New York Public Library 100 Titles for Reading and Sharing selection. And it is, as they say, a Newbery book.

Karen Hesse lives with her husband and two daughters in Williamsville, Vermont.

Unit Objectives
Out of the Dust

1. Through reading **Out of the Dust** by Karen Hesse, students will gain a better understanding of the themes of having a dream, parent/child relationships, friendship, hard work, personal and community values, passion, love, death, loss, and reconciliation.

2. Students will demonstrate their understanding of the text on four levels: factual, interpretive, critical, and personal.

3. Students will define their own viewpoints on the vast number of issues presented in the novel.

4. Students will be exposed to new ways of looking at their own lives and the lives of other people.

5. Students will study various aspects of modern farming and will create plans for dealing with some of the needs of the farming community.

6. Students will be practice reading aloud as well as silently.

7. Students will enrich their vocabularies and improve their understanding of the novel through the vocabulary lessons prepared for use in conjunction with it.

8. Students will practice writing through a variety of assignments.

9. The writing assignments in this unit are geared to several purposes:
   a. to check the students' reading comprehension
   b. to make students think about the ideas presented in the book
   c. to allow students to write from personal experience, to inform, and to persuade
   d. to provide the opportunity to review standard English
   e. to encourage critical and logical thinking

10. Students will be encouraged to make connections between the book and real life.

Reading Assignment Sheet
Out of the Dust

Section of the Text Assigned	Date Assigned	Date to be Completed
Section 1 *Beginning: August 1920* through *Birthday for F.D.R.*		
Section 2 *Not Too Much To Ask* through *Breaking Drought*		
Section 3 *Dazzled* through *Fields of Flashing Light*		
Section 4 *Tested by Dust* through *On the Road with Arley*		
Section 5 *Hope in a Drizzle* through *Devoured*		
Section 6 *Blame* through *The Path of Our Sorrow*		
Section 7 *Hired Work* through *Art Exhibit*		
Section 8 *State Tests Again* through *Outlined by Dust*		
Section 9 *The President's Ball* through *The Competition*		
Section 10 *The Piano Player* through *Following in His Steps*		
Section 11 *Heartsick* through *Blankets of Black*		
Section 12 *The Visit* through *Old Bones*		
Section 13 *The Dream* through *Met*		
Section 14 *Cut It Deep* through *November Dust*		

Unit Outline
Out of the Dust

1 Introduction Distribution Bulletin Board activity	2 PVR #1 Reading aloud Oral reading evaluation	3 Rewriting exercise	4 PVR #2 Reading aloud Preview work homework	5 Checking preview work Read #3 WA #1 (personal exp.)
6 Quiz Finish WA#1 PVR #4	7 Nonfiction Reading Assignment	8 NFRA updates (one interesting fact) PVR #5 (CQ option)	9 PVR #6 (CQ option) Project Modern Farming)	10 PVR #7 WA #2 (to inform)
11 PVR #8 Quiz Metaphor exercise or CQ option	12 Role playing exercise (Character)	13 Review PVR #9 (CQ option)	14 PVR #10 (CQ option) Project updates	15 PVR #11 (CQ option) Finish Project updates
16 PVR #12 Quiz	17 PVR #13 (CQ option)	18 PBR #14 WA #3	19 Review Quiz	20 Discussion using Extra Discussion Questions/Writing Assignments
21 Finishing discussion	22 Vocabulary review	23 Games/puzzles review	24 Unit Testing	

Key: P = Preview Study Questions
V = Vocabulary Work
R = Read
WA = Writing Assignment
CQ option (option to use critical based questions)

STUDY GUIDE QUESTIONS

Short Answer Study Questions
Out of the Dust

WINTER 1934
Section 1: *Beginning: August 1920* through *Birthday for F.D.R.*
1. What were the circumstances of Billie Jo Kelby's birth?
2. Why was the heroin named Billie Jo?
3. What are Mr. Noble and Mr. Romney arguing about in *Rabbit Battles*?
4. In what way does Billie Jo "lose" Livie Killian?
5. Who did Arley Wanderdale ask to play at the Palace before he asked Billie Jo?
6. How does Billie Jo get her mother's permission to play the piano at the Palace?
7. What does Billie Jo say that playing piano can be in *On Stage*?
8. Where does the money collected at the ball in *Birthday for F.D.R.* go?

Section 2: *Not Too Much To Ask* through *Breaking Drought*
1. What did Billie Jo's mother donate to people in need?
2. Why did Billie Jo think she had to be so vigilant about money at Mr. Hardly's store?
3. What did Billie Jo do when it was discovered that Mr. Hardly had given her four extra cents in change?
4. What would Billie Jo's mother have done if Billie Jo had taken a gift from Mr. Hardly?
5. Where did the wind storm take place in *Fifty Miles South of Home*?
6. Why does Billie Jo's family set the table with plates upside down, glasses bottom up, and napkins folded over the silverware?
7. What does Billie Jo's father mean when he says, "The potatoes are peppered plenty tonight, Polly"?
8. What happened in *Breaking Drought* after seventy days?

Section 3: *Dazzled* through *Fields of Flashing Light*
1. About what is Billie Jo dazzled in the poem of that name?
2. What happens to Billie Jo's father when he watches her mother play the piano?
3. When did Billie Jo's mother first teach her to play the piano?
4. What does Billie Jo's mother say is the main reason that Billie Jo's father still believes in rain?
5. Why won't Billie Jo's mother allow her to play for *Sunny of Sunnyside*?
6. What did Billie Jo's mother say when told that Billie Jo scored at the top of the eighth grade at her school on an achievement test?
7. What is the main event that happens in *Fields of Flashing Light*?

Dust Short Answer Study Questions continued page 2

SPRING 1934
Section 4: *Tested by Dust* through *On the Road with Arley*
1. For what reason does Billie Jo think that she and the other students should get bonus points on their six-weeks achievement test?
2. What money is the Kelby family going to get in time for the baby's coming?
3. What bad news does the county agent bring in *Beat Wheat*?
4. Who is Joe De La Flor?
5. What is the major dispute between Billie Jo's mother and father in *Give Up on Wheat*?
6. What opera does Billie Jo realize she has never heard of in *What I Don't Know*?
7. Why are the two apple trees in Billie Jo's yard still alive?
8. What does Billie Jo's father say he remembers about World War I in France?
9. What will happen to the apples on the trees in a couple of months?
10. What was wrong with the rain that came in *Dust and Rain*?
11. How much wheat does Billie Jo think her father will get harvested per acre of land?
12. How does Arley pay Billie Jo for her piano playing?

SUMMER 1934
Section 5: *Hope in a Drizzle* through *Devoured*
1. How much rain fell in *Hope in a Drizzle*?
2. What did Billie Jo secretly watch her mother doing during the light rainfall?
3. What did Billie Jo's mother do when Bill Jo asked what she thought of having five babies all at once like Elzire Dionne in Canada?
4. Where does Billie Jo say that she would like to walk to one day like the boys who are leaving their homes?
5. What was the initial cause of the accident that hurt Billie Jo and her mother?
6. How were Billie Jo's hands hurt during the accident?
7. Who did Doc Rice tend to first when he arrived after the accident?
8. What was the only real thing in Billie Jo's nightmare after the accident?
9. What does Billie Jo say that her mother smells like lying under the sheet tent?
10. What did Billie Jo's father do with the money he found in the house after the accident?
11. What did Billie Jo do to make it worse for her mother while her father was in Guymon?
12. How did Billie Jo's mother die?

Section 6: *Blame* through *The Path of Our Sorrow*
1. Why didn't Billie Jo's Aunt Ellis take the newborn baby back to Lubbock with her?
2. What does Billie Jo hear the women saying about her after her mother's death?
3. Why does Billie Jo sit alone behind Arley Wanderdale's house?
4. What advice does President Roosevelt give the farmers in *Roots*?

Dust Short Answer Study Questions continued page 3

5. What are the empty spaces Billie Jo and her father are trying to fill?
6. Why is Billie Jo's father digging a hole in their yard?
7. What does Billie Jo say she will never be able to forgive her father for as long as she lives?
8. When Billie Jo hears about Kilauea, what does the volcano remind her of?
9. In *Boxes*, what does Billie Jo talk about that she keeps in her closet?
10. What did Mrs. Brown's cereus plant do at midnight on Saturday night and at dawn on Sunday?
11. What does Miss Freeland say the world needed from America right after World War I?
12. How big does Billie Jo say the sorrow is that is upon wheat farmers like her father?

AUTUMN 1934
Section 7: *Hired Work* through *Art Exhibit*
1. Why did Billie Jo's father take a job with Wireless Power?
2. What did the rain do to the sidewalks in town during *Almost Rain*?
3. Who is the only person who talks about Billie Jo's hands now?
4. What made the grass, the wheat, the cattle, the rabbits, and Billie Jo's father happy in *Real Snow*?
5. What doesn't Mad Dog Craddock do that pleases Billie Jo in *Dance Revue*?
6. Why was Mad Dog given that nickname at age two?
7. What was the purpose of the art exhibit held in the basement of the courthouse?

WINTER 1936
Section 8: *State Tests Again* through *Outlined by Dust*
1. What would be enough for Billie Jo to hear now from her mother about the state tests?
2. Why doesn't Billie Jo make cranberry sauce for Christmas dinner the year her mother dies?
3. Why did the county agent shoot Joe De La Flor's cows?
4. What will Joe De La Flor gather to feed his remaining cows in the spring?
5. Why doesn't Billie Jo go to school in *First Rain*?
6. What could Haydon P. Nye see when he first came to Oklahoma?
7. What did Billie Jo see Jim Martin doing at the Crystal Hotel following the rainfall mixed with dust?
8. What two things does Billie Jo notice that she and her father both do the same?
9. How does Billie Jo figure her father "gets the sound of him" instead of talking?
10. What did Billie Jo's mother do to "fit" Billie Jo's father?

Section 9: *The President's Ball* through *The Competition*
1. Where was the dance held that Billie Jo and her father attended?
2. What did the dance raise thirty-three dollars for?
3. What did the government, the bakery, and some local dairy farmers do for the children at the school?
4. Who moved into Billie Jo's school classroom?
5. Why did the children bring the fixings for soup to school?

Dust Short Answer Study Questions continued page 4

6. What did they dress the new baby wear in *Birth*?
7. Which way did the family head when they left Billie Jo's school?
8. What happened to the sugar that Sheriff Robertson found at the still on the Cimarron River?
9. Why is Billie Jo practicing piano again in *Dreams*?
10. What did Billie Jo win in the talent show competition at the Palace?

Section 10: *The Piano Player* through *Following in His Steps*
1. What does Billie Jo especially not want people to say when she plays the piano?
2. What is "no good" in the poem of that name?
3. What did Billie Jo have to check about the snow that fell in *Snow*?
4. What does Billie Jo think is her father's reason for wanting to attend night school?
5. Why does Calb Hardly miss Pete Guymon in *Dust Pneumonia*?
6. After all of the trauma of the dust storm, what does Billie Jo do at the end of the poem of that name?
7. What is the "broken promise" in the poem of that name?
8. Who could make Billie Jo less eager to leave home?
9. What happened to Haydon Parley Nye's widow?

SPRING 1935
Section 11: *Heartsick* through *Blankets of Black*
1. Who is the boy Billie Jo thinks of in *Heartsick*?
2. What marks does Billie Jo's father have on him in *Skin*?
3. Why does Billie Jo say that she should steer clear of Mad Dog Craddock?
4. What subject do people not talk about to Billie Jo's face?
5. What is in the letter that Aunt Ellis sent to Billie Jo's father?
6. Why can't Billie Jo remember the names of the migrant workers who have gone out to California?
7. Whose funeral did Billie Jo and her father set out for?
8. What wouldn't start at the end of *Blankets of Black*?

Section 12: *The Visit* through *Old Bones*
1. What kind of job was Mad Dog hoping to get in Amarillo?
2. Who wound up in a kind of freak show in Ontario?
3. What does Billie Jo's father put on the shelf above the piano besides her mother's book of poetry and her aunt's invitation?
4. What did Miss Freeland do when Billie Jo played the piano at graduation?
5. What started filling up when the rain poured down?
6. What did Billie Jo's father do after it rained and he got the tractor started?
7. Who is singing in his saddle since the rain came?
8. Why can't Billie Jo work for the CCC?
9. What was everybody in town doing at the Joyce City Hardware and Furniture Company on a Sunday afternoon?

Dust Short Answer Study Questions continued page 5

10. What did Harley Madden find at the church one Sunday?
11. Where did Billie Jo find the dimes her mother had saved from the money she earned playing piano?
12. What does Billie Jo's father say when she proposes that they go to see the dinosaur site?

SUMMER 1935
Section 13: *The Dream* through *Met*
1. What does Billie Jo liken the piano to in *The Dream*?
2. Who is the major reason that Billie Jo decides to leave home?
3. What direction does Billie travel in when she leaves home?
4. How does Billie Jo feel after two days on the train?
5. What did the man on the train take when he left Billie Jo?
6. What did Billie Jo think she would do with the picture that the man on the train left behind?
7. Who did Billie Jo call when she got off the train in Flagstaff, Arizona?
8. What did Billie Jo decide wasn't any better, just different?
9. What did Billie Jo call her father when he met her at the train station?
10. What does Billie Jo's father promise to do in *Met*?

AUTUMN 1935
Section 14: *Cut It Deep* through *November Dust*
1. What does Doc Rice tell Billie Jo to do about her hands?
2. What does Billie Jo's father do that is out of the ordinary when Louise comes to dinner?
3. What did Billie Jo do even though she didn't intend to?
4. What is the only thing Billie Jo hopes Louise doesn't do?
5. In *Not Everywhere*, where does Billie Jo not want Louise to go with her and her father?
6. What does Billie Jo like best about Louise?
7. What is "holding its own" in *November Dust*?
8. What are the poppies doing in *Thanksgiving List*?
9. Why does Billie Jo think she is what she is?
10. How did Louise and Billie Jo's father meet?
11. How did Billie Jo's father let her mother know he intended to marry Louise?
12. What was Louise's betrothal gift to Billie Jo's father?

Key: Short Answer Study Questions
Out of the Dust

WINTER 1934
Section 1: *Beginning: August 1920* through *Birthday for F.D.R.*
1. What were the circumstances of Billie Jo Kelby's birth?
    Billie Jo was born at home on the kitchen floor.

2. Why was the heroine of **Out of the Dust** named Billie Jo?
    She was named Billie Jo because her father wanted a boy.

3. What are Mr. Noble and Mr. Romney arguing about in *Rabbit Battles*?
    They are arguing about who can kill the most rabbits.

4. In what way does Billie Jo "lose" Livie Killian?
    Livie Killian moves away with her family.

5. Who did Arley Wanderdale ask to play at the Palace before he asked Billie Jo?
    Arley Wanderdale asked Mad Dog Craddock before he asked Billie Jo.

6. How does Billie Jo get her mother's permission to play the piano at the Palace?
    She asks for permission when her mother has her mind on other things.

7. What does Billie Jo say that playing piano can be in *On Stage*?
    She says it can be supremely heaven.

8. Where does the money collected at the ball in *Birthday for F.D.R.* go?
    The money goes to the Warm Springs Foundation.

Section 2: *Not Too Much To Ask* through *Breaking Drought*
1. What did Billie Jo's mother donate to people in need?
    Her mother donated three jars of applesauce, some cured pork, and a feed-sack nightie she had sewn for her coming baby.
2. Why did Billie Jo think she had to be so vigilant about money at Mr. Hardly's store?
    She had to be vigilant because Mr. Hardly shortchanged customers when he could get away with it.
3. What did Billie Jo do when it was discovered that Mr. Hardly had given her four extra cents in change?
    Billie Jo walked back to the store and returned the money.

Dust Key: Short Answer Study Questions continued page 2

4. What would Billie Jo's mother have done if Billie Jo had taken a gift from Mr. Hardly?
   Her mother would have thrown a fit.
5. Where did the wind storm take place in *Fifty Miles South of Home*?
   The wind storm took place in Amarillo.
6. Why does Billie Jo's family set the table with plates upside down, glasses bottom up, and napkins folded over the silverware?
   They set the table that way because of the dust.
7. What does Billie Jo's father mean when he says, "The potatoes are peppered plenty tonight, Polly"?
   He means that there is dust in the potatoes.
8. What happened in *Breaking Drought* after seventy days?
   After seventy days, it rained a little.

Section 3: *Dazzled* through *Fields of Flashing Light*
1. About what is Billie Jo dazzled in the poem of that name?
   Billie Jo is dazzled by the way her mother plays the piano.
2. What happens to Billie Jo's father when he watches her mother play the piano?
   Her father gets "soft eyes."
3. When did Billie Jo's mother first teach her to play the piano?
   Her mother taught her to play the piano when she was five years old.
4. What does Billie Jo's mother say is the main reason that Billie Jo's father still believes in rain?
   She says he still believes in rain because spring is coming on and he's a farmer.
5. Why won't Billie Jo's mother allow her to play for *Sunny of Sunnyside*?
   She won't allow her to play because it would involve missing school.
6. What did Billie Jo's mother say when told that Billie Jo scored at the top of the eighth grade at her school on an achievement test?
   Her mother said, "I knew you could."
7. What is the main event that happens in *Fields of Flashing Light*?
   The main event is a dust storm.

SPRING 1934
Section 4: *Tested by Dust* through *On the Road with Arley*
1. For what reason does Billie Jo think that she and the other students should get bonus points on their six-weeks achievement test?
   She thinks they should get extra points for testing in a dust storm.
2. What money is the Kelby family going to get in time for the baby's coming?
   They are going to get their own money back after the banks closed.
3. What bad news does the county agent bring in *Beat Wheat*?
   The county agent brings the news that one quarter of the county wheat is lost.
4. Who is Joe De La Flor?
   Joe De La Flor is a neighbor of the Kelby family's.

Dust Key: Short Answer Study Questions continued page 3

5. What is the major dispute between Billie Jo's mother and father in *Give Up on Wheat*?
   She thinks he should put in a pond or try some other crops, and he wants to stick with wheat.
6. What opera does Billie Jo realize she has never heard of in *What I Don't Know*?
   The opera Billie Jo realizes she has never heard of is *Madame Butterfly*.
7. Why are the two apple trees in Billie Jo's yard still alive?
   The apple trees are alive because Billie Jo's mother has nursed them.
8. What does Billie Jo's father say he remembers about World War I in France?
   Billie Jo's father remembers the poppies red on the graves of the dead.
9. What will happen to the apples on the trees in a couple of months?
   In a couple of months the apples will ripen.
10. What was wrong with the rain that came in *Dust and Rain*?
    The rain came too hard.
11. How much wheat does Billie Jo think her father will get harvested per acre of land?
    She thinks he will get no more than five bushels to his acre.
12. How does Arley pay Billie Jo for her piano playing?
    He pays her in dimes.

SUMMER 1934
Section 5: *Hope in a Drizzle* through *Devoured*
1. How much rain fell in *Hope in a Drizzle*?
   A quarter inch of rain fell.
2. What did Billie Jo secretly watch her mother doing during the light rainfall?
   She watched her mother standing naked in the rain.
3. What did Billie Jo's mother do when Billie Jo asked what she thought of having five babies all at once like Elzire Dionne in Canada?
   Her mother wept just to think of it.
4. Where does Billie Jo say that she would like to walk to one day like the boys who are leaving their homes?
   She says she would like to walk her way West.
5. What was the initial cause of the accident that hurt Billie Jo and her mother?
   The initial cause was that Billie Jo's father left a pail of kerosene sitting near the stove.
6. How were Billie Jo's hands hurt during the accident?
   When kerosene from the pail she carried splashed on her mother, Billie Jo tried to beat the flames out.
7. Who did Doc Rice tend to first when he arrived after the accident?
   Doc Rice first tended to Billie Jo's mother.
8. What was the only real thing in Billie Jo's nightmare after the accident?
   Her burned hands were the only real thing in her nightmare.

Dust Key: Short Answer Study Questions continued page 4

9. What does Billie Jo say that her mother smells like lying under the sheet tent?
   She says her mother smells like scorched meat.
10. What did Billie Jo's father do with the money he found in the house after the accident?
    He went out and drank all evening.
11. What did Billie Jo do to make it worse for her mother while her father was in Guymon?
    She tried to give her mother some water and spilled it on her because of her burned hands.
12. How did Billie Jo's mother die?
    Billie Jo's mother died giving birth to a son.

Section 6: *Blame* through *The Path of Our Sorrow*
1. Why didn't Billie Jo's Aunt Ellis take the newborn baby back to Lubbock with her?
   Her Aunt Ellis didn't take the baby back to Lubbock because the child died before she arrived at the Kelbys' home.
2. What does Billie Jo hear the women saying about her after her mother's death?
   She hears them saying, "Billie Jo threw the pail."
3. Why does Billie Jo sit alone behind Arley Wanderdale's house?
   She sits alone and listens to Arley play the piano.
4. What advice does President Roosevelt give the farmers in *Roots*?
   President Roosevelt says they should plant trees.
5. What are the empty spaces Billie Jo and her father are trying to fill?
   They are trying to fill the empty spaces left by Billie Jo's mother.
6. Why is Billie Jo's father digging a hole in their yard?
   He is digging a hole to build the pond that Billie Jo's mother wanted.
7. What does Billie Jo say she will never be able to forgive her father for as long as she lives?
   She says she will never be able to forgive him for leaving the pail of kerosene near the stove.
8. When Billie Jo hears about Kilauea, what does the volcano remind her of?
   The volcano reminds her of a dust storm.
9. In *Boxes*, what does Billie Jo talk about that she keeps in her closet?
   She keeps two boxes of mementos in her closet.
10. What did Mrs. Brown's cereus plant do at midnight on Saturday night and at dawn on Sunday?
    The cereus plant bloomed at midnight and wilted and died at dawn.
11. What does Miss Freeland say the world needed from America right after World War I?
    She says the world needed America's wheat.

Dust Key: Short Answer Study Questions continued page 5

12. How big does Billie Jo say the sorrow is that is upon wheat farmers like her father?
    She says the sorrow is big as Texas.

AUTUMN 1934
Section 7: *Hired Work* through *Art Exhibit*
1. Why did Billie Jo's father take a job with Wireless Power?
    He takes the job with Wireless Power to earn some extra money.
2. What did the rain do to the sidewalks in town during *Almost Rain*?
    The rain only got the sidewalks damp.
3. Who is the only person who talks about Billie Jo's hands now?
    The only person who talks about Billie Jo's hands now is Arley Wanderdale.
4. What made the grass, the wheat, the cattle, the rabbits, and Billie Jo's father happy in *Real Snow*?
    The falling snow made the grass, the wheat, the cattle, the rabbits, and Billie Jo's father happy.
5. What doesn't Mad Dog Craddock do that pleases Billie Jo in *Dance Revue*?
    He doesn't look at her with pity.
6. Why was Mad Dog given that nickname at age two?
    He was given the name because he would bite anything he could catch hold of.
7. What was the purpose of the art exhibit held in the basement of the courthouse?
    The purpose of the art exhibit was to raise money to benefit the library.

WINTER 1936
Section 8: *State Tests Again* through *Outlined by Dust*
1. What would be enough for Billie Jo to hear now from her mother about the state tests?
    It would be enough to hear her say, "I knew you could."
2. Why doesn't Billie Jo make cranberry sauce for Christmas dinner the year her mother dies?
    She doesn't make cranberry sauce because her mother never taught her how.
3. Why did the county agent shoot Joe De La Flor's cows?
    The county agent shot the cows because Joe De La Flor couldn't afford to feed his cows and couldn't afford to sell them.
4. What will Joe De La Flor gather to feed his remaining cows in the spring?
    Joe will gather Russian thistle to feed his remaining cows.
5. Why doesn't Billie Jo go to school in *First Rain*?
    She doesn't go to school because she just wants to stand in the rain.
6. What could Haydon P. Nye see when he first came to Oklahoma?
    When Haydon first came to Oklahoma, he could see only grass, wild horses, and wolves roaming.

Dust Key: Short Answer Study Questions continued page 6

7. What did Billie Jo see Jim Martin doing at the Crystal Hotel following the rainfall mixed with dust?
   She sees Jim Martin scraping up mud that had dried to crust after the rain mixed with dust.
8. What two things does Billie Jo notice that she and her father both do the same?
   They both rub their eyes with their palms out and they both wipe milk from their upper lips with thumb and forefinger.
9. How does Billie Jo figure her father "gets the sound out of him" instead of talking?
   She thinks he does it with the songs he sings.
10. What did Billie Jo's mother do to "fit" Billie Jo's father?
    She made herself over to fit him.

Section 9: *The President's Ball* through *The Competition*
1. Where was the dance held that Billie Jo and her father attended?
   The dance was held at the Legion Hall.
2. What did the dance raise thirty-three dollars for?
   The dance raised thirty-three dollars for infantile paralysis.
3. What did the government, the bakery, and some local dairy farmers do for the children at the school?
   They provided the children at the school with a filling meal.
4. Who moved into Billie Jo's school classroom?
   A family moved into Billie Jo's school classroom.
5. Why did the children bring the fixings for soup to school?
   The children brought the fixings for soup to share with the family at lunch.
6. What did the new baby wear in *Birth*?
   They dressed the baby in a feed-sack nightgown that was Billie Jo's brother's.
7. Which way did the family head when they left Billie Jo's school?
   The family headed west when they left.
8. What happened to the sugar that Sheriff Robertson found at the still on the Cimarron River?
   Sheriff Robertson gave it to Miss Freeland to make sweet things for the children to eat.
9. Why is Billie Jo practicing piano again in *Dreams*?
   She is practicing for the contest being held at the Palace.
10. What did Billie Jo win in the talent show competition at the Palace?
    She won third prize and one dollar.

Dust Key: Short Answer Study Questions continued page 7

Section 10: *The Piano Player* through *Following in His Steps*
1. What does Billie Jo especially not want people to say when she plays the piano?
    She doesn't want them to say, "Billie Jo Kelby plays like a cripple."
2. What is "no good" in the poem of that name?
    Billie Jo's piano playing is no good.
3. What did Billie Jo have to check about the snow that fell in *Snow*?
    She had to check to make sure the snow wasn't dust.
4. What does Billie Jo think is her father's reason for wanting to attend night school?
    She thinks he wants to attend night school to spend time with the ladies there.
5. Why does Calb Hardly miss Pete Guymon in *Dust Pneumonia*?
    Calb Hardly misses Pete because Pete used to joke with him and ask about the Wildcats.
6. After all of the trauma of the dust storm, what does Billie Jo do at the end of the poem of that name?
    She turns the plates and glasses upside down, crawls into bed, and sleeps.
7. What is the "broken promise" in the poem of that name?
    The broken promise is that it rained a little everywhere but in Billie Jo's neighborhood.
8. Who could make Billie Jo less eager to leave home?
    Billie Jo's mother could make her less eager to leave home.
9. What happened to Haydon Parley Nye's widow?
    She died two months after Haydon did.

SPRING 1935

Section 11: *Heartsick* through *Blankets of Black*
1. Who is the boy Billie Jo thinks of in *Heartsick*?
    The boy she thinks of is Mad Dog Craddock.
2. What marks does Billie Jo's father have on him in *Skin*?
    He has raised spots on his nose, cheek, and neck.
3. Why does Billie Jo say that she should steer clear of Mad Dog Craddock?
    She says that she should steer clear of him because she's had enough of quiet men.
4. What subject do people not talk about to Billie Jo's face?
    No one talks about fire to Billie Jo's face.
5. What is in the letter that Aunt Ellis sent to Billie Jo's father?
    In the letter was an invitation for Billie Jo to come and live with her in Lubbock.
6. Why can't Billie Jo remember the names of the migrant workers who have gone out to California?
    She can't remember their names because there are too many of them.
7. Whose funeral did Billie Jo and her father set out for?
    The funeral was that of Grandma Lucas.

Dust Short Answer Study Questions continued page 8

8. What wouldn't start at the end of *Blankets of Black*?
   The truck wouldn't start.

Section 12: *The Visit* through *Old Bones*
1. What kind of job was Mad Dog hoping to get in Amarillo?
   Mad Dog was hoping to get a job singing on the radio.
2. Who wound up in a kind of freak show?
   The Dionne Quintuplets wound up in a kind of freak show.
3. What does Billie Jo's father put on the shelf above the piano beside her mother's book of poetry and her aunt's invitation?
   He put the papers about his government loan on the shelf.
4. What did Miss Freeland do when Billie Jo played the piano at graduation?
   Miss Freeland started to cry.
5. What started filling up when the rain poured down?
   Billie Jo's father's near-finished pond started filling up.
6. What did Billie Jo's father do after it rained and he got the tractor started?
   He drove the tractor out to the fields.
7. Who is singing in his saddle since the rain came?
   Joe De La Flor is singing in his saddle.
8. Why can't Billie Jo work for the CCC?
   She can't work for the CCC because she is too young and the wrong sex.
9. What was everybody in town doing at the Joyce City Hardware and Furniture Company on a Sunday afternoon?
   They were listening to Mad Dog Craddock sing in Amarillo.
10. What did Harley Madden find at the church one Sunday?
    Harley found a baby at the church.
11. Where did Billie Jo find the dimes her mother had saved from the money she earned playing piano?
    She found the dimes inside an envelope in the box of her baby brother's nighties.
12. What does Billie Jo's father say when she proposes that they go to see the dinosaur site?
    He says, "It's best to let the dead rest."

SUMMER 1935
Section 13: *The Dream* through *Met*
1. What does Billie Jo liken the piano to in *The Dream*?
   She likens the piano to her mother.
2. Who is the major reason that Billie Jo decides to leave home?
   Her father is the major reason she decides to leave home.
3. What direction does Billie Jo travel in when she leaves home?
   When she leaves home, Billie Jo heads west.

Dust Short Answer Study Questions continued page 9

4. How does Billie Jo feel after two days on the train?
   She felt stiff and sore.
5. What did the man on the train take when he left Billie Jo?
   The man on the train took Billie Jo's remaining biscuits.
6. What did Billie Jo think she would do with the picture that the man on the train left behind?
   She thought she would send it to the man's family to let them know he was still alive.
7. Who did Billie Jo call when she got off the train in Flagstaff, Arizona?
   She called her father.
8. What did Billie Jo decide wasn't any better, just different?
   She decided that getting away wasn't any better, just different.
9. What did Billie Jo call her father when he met her at the train station?
   She called her father "Daddy."
10. What does Billie Jo's father promise to do in *Met*?
    He promises to see Doc Rice about his skin problem.

AUTUMN 1935
Section 14: *Cut It Deep* through *November Dust*
1. What does Doc Rice tell Billie Jo to do about her hands?
   Doc Rice tells Billie Jo to quit picking at them, put ointment on them, and use them.
2. What does Billie Jo's father do that is out of the ordinary when Louise comes to dinner?
   Billie Jo's father cleans up after dinner.
3. What did Billie Jo do even though she didn't intend to?
   She likes Louise even though she didn't intend to.
4. What is the only thing Billie Jo hopes Louise doesn't do?
   She hopes that Louise doesn't crowd her out of her father's life.
5. In *Not Everywhere*, where does Billie Jo not want Louise to go with her and her father?
   She doesn't want Louise to go with her and her father to visit her mother and the baby's grave.
6. What does Billie Jo like best about Louise?
   What she likes best is that Louise doesn't tell her what to do but just nods.
7. What is "holding its own" in *November Dust*?
   The pond that her father dug is holding its own.
8. What are the poppies doing in *Thanksgiving List*?
   The poppies are blooming on the grave of Billie Jo's mother and the baby.

Dust Short Answer Study Questions continued page 10

9. Why does Billie Jo think she is what she is?
    She thinks she is what she is because of the dust.
10. How did Louise and Billie Jo's father meet?
    Louise was Billie Jo's father's night school teacher.
11. How did Billie Jo's father let her mother know he intended to marry Louise?
    Her father went to the gravesite and informed her of his intentions.
12. What was Louise's betrothal gift to Billie Jo's father?
    Louise's gift was a second mule.

Multiple Choice Quizzes
Out of the Dust

WINTER 1934

Section 1: *Beginning: August 1920* through *Birthday for F.D.R.*

1. What were the circumstances of Billie Jo Kelby's birth?
    a. She was born in the new hospital in Amarillo.
    b. She was born in a taxicab on the way to the hospital.
    c. She was born in the barn during a dust storm.
    d. She was born at home on the kitchen floor.

2. Why was the heroine named Billie Jo?
    a. Because she looked like a country singer
    b. Because that was her grandmother's name
    c. Because her father wanted a boy
    d. Because that was the name of her mother's childhood friend

3. What are Mr. Noble and Mr. Romney arguing about in *Rabbit Battles*?
    a. The price of wheat
    b. Mr. Hardly's handling of money
    c. Who can kill more rabbits
    d. Who will kill the first rabbit that year

4. In what way does Billie Jo "lose" Livie Killian?
    a. Livie moves away with her family.
    b. She and Livie have a big argument.
    c. Livie dies.
    d. Livie wanders away from home and is never found.

5. Who did Arley Wanderdale ask to play at the Palace before he asked Billie Jo?
    a. He asked Billie Jo's mother.
    b. He asked Mad Dog Craddock.
    c. He asked Miss Freeland.
    d. He asked his wife, Vera.

6. How does Billie Jo get her mother's permission to play the piano at the Palace?
    a. She asks for permission when her mother has her mind on other things.
    b. She offers to do chores in return for permission to play.
    c. She makes her mother feel guilty.
    d. She offers to do homework twice as long each night to make up for the time she spends on piano practice.

Dust Multiple Choice Quizzes continued page 2

7. What does Billie Jo say that playing piano can be in *On Stage*?
    a. She says it can be wonderful.
    b. She says it can be thrilling.
    c. She says it can be supremely heaven.
    d. She says it can be heaven on earth.

8. Where does the money collected at the ball in *Birthday for F.D.R.* go?
    a. The Warm Springs Foundation
    b. Infantile paralysis
    c. The Heart Association
    d. The local library

Dust Multiple Choice Quizzes continued page 3

Section 2: *Not Too Much To Ask* through *Breaking Drought*

1. What did Billie Jo's mother donate to people in need?
    a. An old coat of hers
    b. Three jars of applesauce, some cured pork, and a feed-sack nightie she had sewn for her coming baby
    c. A chicken and some potatoes
    d. Some of Billie Jo's old clothing

2. Why did Billie Jo think she had to be so vigilant about money at Mr. Hardly's store?
    a. Because she had trouble with arithmetic
    b. Because Mr. Hardly shortchanged customers when he could get away with it
    c. Because she carried her money in one pocket and her mother's in another
    d. Because Mr. Hardly got mixed up when he counted

3. What did Billie Jo do when it was discovered that Mr. Hardly had given her four extra cents in change?
    a. She bought some sheet music with the extra money.
    b. She gave it to her mother to put in the bank.
    c. She walked back to the store and returned the money.
    d. She reminded herself to take it back to him the next time she went to the store.

4. What would Billie Jo's mother have done if Billie Jo had taken a gift from Mr. Hardly?
    a. She would have made Billie Jo return it.
    b. She would have laughed.
    c. She would have told Billie Jo's father.
    d. She would have thrown a fit.

5. Where did the wind storm take place in *Fifty Miles South of Home*?
    a. In Texhoma
    b. In Enid
    c. In Amarillo
    d. In Joyce City

6. Why does Billie Jo's family set the table with plates upside down, glasses bottom up, and napkins folded over the silverware?
    a. Because of the dust
    b. Because it is a family ritual
    c. Because they set the table at night
    d. Because her father likes it that way

Dust Multiple Choice Quizzes continued page 4

7. What does Billie Jo's father mean when he says, "The potatoes are peppered plenty tonight, Polly"?
    a. He means that Billie Jo's mother has spoiled the meal again.
    b. He means that she forgot to put pepper on the potatoes.
    c. He means that there is dust on the potatoes.
    d. He is just making a little joke between them.

8. What happened in *Breaking Drought* after seventy days?
    a. It poured for three whole days.
    b. It rained a little.
    c. It rained hard for an hour and then stopped.
    d. It snowed.

Dust Multiple Choice Quizzes continued page 5

Section 3: *Dazzled* through *Fields of Flashing Light*

1. About what is Billie Jo dazzled in the poem of that name?
    a. By the way her mother plays the piano
    b. By the way Mad Dog talks to her
    c. By the way her father talks about wheat
    d. By the way her mother and father look at each other

2. What happens to Billie Jo's father when he watches her mother play the piano?
    a. He gets "soft eyes."
    b. He gets angry with her.
    c. He remembers their courtship.
    d. He worries that she will leave him.

3. When did Billie Jo's mother first teach her to play the piano?
    a. When Billie Jo was eighteen months old
    b. When Billie Jo was five
    c. When Billie Jo was ten
    d. When Billie Jo was twelve

4. What does Billie Jo's mother say is the main reason that Billie Jo's father still believes in rain?
    a. Because he is foolish
    b. Because he is a Kelby
    c. Because spring is coming and he's a farmer
    d. Because he has no idea how to be a farmer

5. Why won't Billie Jo's mother allow her to play for *Sunny of Sunnyside*?
    a. Because she is jealous of Billie Jo's talent
    b. Because playing would mean Billie Jo would be up too late
    c. Because she wants to keep Billie Jo away from Mad Dog Craddock
    d. Because it would involve missing school

6. What did Billie Jo's mother say when told that Billie Jo scored at the top of the eighth grade at her school on an achievement test?
    a. "Very good, Billie Jo."
    b. "Great going, girl."
    c. "I knew you could."
    d. "I didn't think you had it in you."

Dust Multiple Choice Quizzes continued page 6

7. What is the main event that happens in *Fields of Flashing Light*?
    a. A meteor shower
    b. A snow storm
    c. A rain storm
    d. A dust storm

Dust Multiple Choice Quizzes continued page 7

SPRING 1934
Section 4: *Tested by Dust* through *On the Road with Arley*
1. For what reason does Billie Jo think that she and the other students should get bonus points on their six-weeks achievement test?
    a. For doing so well on the test
    b. For performing well even though they were hungry
    c. For testing in a dust storm
    d. For testing so well even though they had no practice test

2. What money is the Kelby family going to get in time for the baby's coming?
    a. Their own money back after the banks closed
    b. A big refund on their income taxes
    c. Money that a neighbor owed them
    d. Money inherited from Billie Jo's grandmother

3. What bad news does the county agent bring in *Beat Wheat*?
    a. There is no wheat seed in the whole county.
    b. One quarter of the county wheat is lost.
    c. The price of wheat is falling fast.
    d. Nobody seems to want to buy wheat.

4. Who is Joe De La Flor?
    a. He is the singing cowboy on the local radio station.
    b. He is a neighbor of the Kelby family's.
    c. He is an old boyfriend of Billie Jo's mother's.
    d. He is the owner of the local grocery store.

5. What is the major dispute between Billie Jo's mother and father in *Give Up on Wheat*?
    a. She wants to move west, and he wants to stay put.
    b. She wants to raise sugar cane, and he wants to raise barley.
    c. She wants him to cut back on the wheat he grows.
    d. She thinks he should put in a pond or try some other crops, and he wants to stick with wheat.

6. What opera does Billie Jo realize she has never heard of in *What I Don't Know*?
    a. Wagner's The Rings
    b. Madame Butterfly
    c. Carmen
    d. West Side Story

Dust Multiple Choice Quizzes continued page 8

7. Why are the two apple trees in Billie Jo's yard still alive?
   a. Because they are a very hardy variety
   b. Because Billie Jo's father cares for them
   c. Because Billie Jo's mother has nursed them
   d. Nobody really knows why.

8. What does Billie Jo's father say he remembers about World War I in France?
   a. All of the dead soldiers
   b. The great food offered by the French people
   c. The poppies red on the graves of the dead
   d. The great wine

9. What will happen to the apples on the trees in a couple of months?
   a. They will be blown off the trees by a dust storm.
   b. They will still be too green to eat.
   c. They will turn yellow and fall to the ground.
   d. They will ripen.

10. What was wrong with the rain that came in *Dust and Rain*?
    a. The rain was too short.
    b. The rain turned to snow.
    c. The rain turned to sleet.
    d. The rain came too hard.

11. How much wheat does Billie Jo think her father will get harvested per acre of land?
    a. At least fifty bushels to his acre
    b. No more than fifty-five bushels to his acre
    c. No more than five bushels to his acre
    d. Probably ten bushels to his acre

12. How does Arley pay Billie Jo for her piano playing?
    a. He tutors her in math.
    b. He gives her fifty cents before playing and fifty cents after.
    c. He pays her in dimes.
    d. He gives her a crisp dollar bill each time she plays.

Dust Multiple Choice Quizzes continued page 9

SUMMER 1934
Section 5: *Hope in a Drizzle* through *Devoured*

1. How much rain fell in *Hope in a Drizzle*?
    a. Ten inches
    b. A quarter inch
    c. Four inches
    d. A half inch

2. What did Billie Jo secretly watch her mother doing during the light rainfall?
    a. Singing in the parlor
    b. Smiling at Billie Jo's father
    c. Standing naked in the rain
    d. Smiling secretly at Joe De La Flor

3. What did Billie Jo's mother do when Bill Jo asked what she thought of having five babies all at once like Elzire Dionne in Canada?
    a. She said she envied Elzire Dionne.
    b. She wept just to think of it.
    c. She laughed.
    d. She smiled.

4. Where does Billie Jo say that she would like to walk to one day like the boys who are leaving their homes?
    a. At least to Amarillo
    b. Her way West
    c. East to the White House
    d. All the way into Texas

5. What was the initial cause of the accident that hurt Billie Jo and her mother?
    a. The fire was too hot.
    b. Her father left a pail of kerosene sitting near the stove.
    c. The pot of water boiled over.
    d. Her mother turned the pail of kerosene over.

6. How were Billie Jo's hands hurt during the accident?
    a. Her mother spilled the kerosene on Billie Jo.
    b. When kerosene from the pail she carried splashed on her mother, Billie Jo tried to beat the flames out.
    c. She slipped and fell and knocked the pail of kerosene on herself.
    d. When everybody started yelling, Billie Jo slipped and knocked the pail of kerosene over.

Dust Multiple Choice Quizzes continued page 10

7. Who did Doc Rice tend to first when he arrived after the accident?
   a. Billie Jo's father
   b. The horses
   c. Billie Jo's mother
   d. Billie Jo

8. What was the only real thing in Billie Jo's nightmare after the accident?
   a. Her mother's face
   b. Her father's angry looks
   c. Her burned hands
   d. Her mother's moans

9. What does Billie Jo say that her mother smells like lying under the sheet tent?
   a. Something stinking
   b. A bad dream
   c. Scorched meat
   d. Rotten eggs

10. What did Billie Jo's father do with the money he found in the house after the accident?
    a. He paid for Billie Jo's mother's funeral.
    b. He bought Billie Jo a black dress to wear to the funeral.
    c. He went out and drank all evening.
    d. He put the money in the bank.

11. What did Billie Jo do to make it worse for her mother while her father was in Guymon?
    a. She wouldn't give her mother any water.
    b. She tried to give her mother some water and spilled it on her because of her burned hands.
    c. She touched her mother's burned body.
    d. She tried to turn her mother over to make her more comfortable.

12. How did Billie Jo's mother die?
    a. She never survived the accident.
    b. She had a heart attack.
    c. She died giving birth to a son.
    d. She went into shock and died.

Dust Multiple Choice Quizzes continued page 11

Section 6: *Blame* through *The Path of Our Sorrow*

1. Why didn't Billie Jo's Aunt Ellis take the newborn baby back to Lubbock with her?
    a. Because Billie Jo's father wouldn't let her
    b. Because Billie Jo cried to keep the baby
    c. Because the child died before she arrived at the Kelbys' home
    d. Because she decided that the baby should be with his father

2. What does Billie Jo hear the women saying about her after her mother's death?
    a. "Billie Jo just doesn't know any better."
    b. "Billie Jo should go and live with her Aunt Ellis."
    c. "Billie Jo has no feelings at all."
    d. "Billie Jo threw the pail."

3. Why does Billie Jo sit alone behind Arley Wanderdale's house?
    a. Because she thinks of Mad Dog there
    b. Because Arley's house reminds her of her mother
    c. Because she sits alone and listens to Arley play the piano
    d. Because she enjoys the wooded area behind his house

4. What advice does President Roosevelt give the farmers in *Roots*?
    a. Go West
    b. Raise more wheat
    c. Trust in God
    d. Plant trees

5. What are the empty spaces Billie Jo and her father are trying to fill?
    a. The long gaps in their conversations
    b. The great difference in their ages
    c. The empty spaces left by Billie Jo's mother
    d. The bad feelings between them

6. Why is Billie Jo's father digging a hole in their yard?
    a. Because he wants to die
    b. To fill the pond Billie Jo's mother wanted
    c. To bury the animals lost in the dust storm
    d. Because he wants to show how manly he is

Dust Multiple Choice Quizzes continued page 12

7. What does Billie Jo say she will never be able to forgive her father for as long as she lives?
    a. Leaving the pail of kerosene near the stove
    b. Going off and drinking
    c. Not talking to her about her mother
    d. Not praising her

8. When Billie Jo hears about Kilauea, what does the volcano remind her of?
    a. Her father's violent nature
    b. A dust storm
    c. A firecracker, only bigger
    d. Life in Oklahoma

9. In *Boxes*, what does Billie Jo talk about that she keeps in her closet?
    a. Two boxes of mementos
    b. Hats that were her mother's stored in hat boxes
    c. The money that she has made
    d. Pictures of Mad Dog Craddock

10. What did Mrs. Brown's cereus plant do at midnight on Saturday night and at dawn on Sunday?
    a. It closed its leaves and then opened them.
    b. It started to bloom and then stopped completely.
    c. It bloomed and stopped and then started again at dawn
    d. It bloomed at midnight and wilted and died at dawn.

11. What does Miss Freeland say the world needed from America right after World War I?
    a. More heart
    b. Courage
    c. America's wheat
    d. A rest

12. How big does Billie Jo say the sorrow is that is upon wheat farmers like her father?
    a. Bigger than a bread box
    b. Big as Texas
    c. Big enough to do them all in
    d. Bigger than life

Dust Multiple Choice Quizzes continued page 13

AUTUMN 1934
Section 7: *Hired Work* through *Art Exhibit*
1. Why did Billie Jo's father take a job with Wireless Power?
    a. He couldn't stand sitting around the house anymore.
    b. He had always wanted to have a job with a power company.
    c. He didn't like sitting around listening to Billie Jo talk.
    d. He did it to earn some money.

2. What did the rain do to the sidewalks in town during *Almost Rain*?
    a. It gave them a real soaking.
    b. It made them slippery.
    c. It only got them damp.
    d. It made them look slightly oily.

3. Who is the only person who talks about Billie Jo's hands now?
    a. Arley Wanderdale
    b. Her father
    c. Mad Dog Craddock
    d. Miss Freeland

4. What made the grass, the wheat, the cattle, the rabbits, and Billie Jo's father happy in *Real Snow*?
    a. The falling rain
    b. The sun shining on the new snow
    c. The falling snow
    d. The bright sunshine after the snow

5. What doesn't Mad Dog Craddock do that pleases Billie Jo in *Dance Revue*?
    a. He doesn't dance with any other girls.
    b. He doesn't brag about himself.
    c. He doesn't look at her with pity.
    d. He doesn't stare at her hands.

6. Why was Mad Dog given that nickname at age two?
    a. Because he behaved like a rabid dog
    b. Because he would bite anything he could catch hold of
    c. Because he acted foolish
    d. Because he snarled like a wild animal

Dust Multiple Choice Quizzes continued page 14

7. What was the purpose of the art exhibit held in the basement of the courthouse?
    a. To raise money to benefit the library
    b. To raise money for heart disease
    c. To show visitors that Joyce City had talent too
    d. To show off an exhibit from Amarillo

Dust Multiple Choice Quizzes continued page 15

WINTER 1936
Section 8: *State Tests Again* through *Outlined by Dust*

1. What would be enough for Billie Jo to hear now from her mother about the state tests?
    a. "There, there, Billie Jo. You did well."
    b. "Good job, Billie Jo."
    c. "I knew you could."
    d. "Congratulations."

2. Why doesn't Billie Jo make cranberry sauce for Christmas dinner the year her mother dies?
    a. Because it just doesn't seem worth it for just her and her father.
    b. Because her mother never taught her how
    c. Because they only have cranberry sauce when company comes
    d. Because they have enough to eat already

3. Why did the county agent shoot Joe De La Flor's cows?
    a. Because he was angry
    b. Because Joe couldn't afford to feed his cows and couldn't afford to sell them
    c. Because Joe had fallen behind in his taxes
    d. Because the cows were very ill

4. What will Joe De La Flor gather to feed his remaining cows in the spring?
    a. He will gather Russian thistle for them.
    b. He will get together all the dimes in the house and cash them in
    c. He will gather some bales of hay.
    d. He will gather his friends and ask them for help.

5. Why doesn't Billie Jo go to school in *First Rain*?
    a. Because she just wants to stand in the rain
    b. Because she doesn't own a rain coat
    c. Because she has no nice clothes to wear
    d. Because she suddenly turned her attention elsewhere

6. What could Haydon P. Nye see when he first came to Oklahoma?
    a. Oil fields
    b. Only grass, wild horses, and wolves roaming
    c. His future wife
    d. The prospects of growing wheat

Dust Multiple Choice Quizzes continued page 16

7. What did Billie Jo see Jim Martin doing at the Crystal Hotel following the rainfall mixed with dust?
   a. Scraping up mud that had dried to crust after the rain mixed
   b. Wiping up the mud that had gotten tracked in
   c. Cleaning up the front windows
   d. Singing to himself

8. What two things does Billie Jo notice that she and her father both do the same?
   a. Eat crackers and drink milk right from the jug
   b. Rub their eyes with their palms out and wipe milk from their upper lips with thumb and forefinger
   c. Sing and smile
   d. Laugh and cry

9. How does Billie Jo figure her father "gets the sound of him" instead of talking?
   a. With the songs he sings
   b. By humming while he works
   c. With the thinking he does all day
   d. By pretending to talk to someone close by

10. What did Billie Jo's mother do to "fit" Billie Jo's father?
    a. She pretended to like farm life.
    b. She pretended to love him.
    c. She made herself over to fit him.
    d. She took a farm extension course.

Dust Multiple Choice Quizzes continued page 17

Section 9: *The President's Ball* through *The Competition*

1. Where was the dance held that Billie Jo and her father attended?
    a. At a big hotel downtown
    b. At the Legion hall
    c. At a local park
    d. At Billie Jo's school

2. What did the dance raise thirty-three dollars for?
    a. The Heart Association
    b. A poor family locally
    c. Infantile paralysis
    d. Tobacco related diseases

3. What did the government, the bakery, and some local dairy farmers do for the children?
    a. They provided the children with a filling meal.
    b. They gave them all food to take home to their families.
    c. They gave the children lessons in agriculture.
    d. They entered a food contest at Billie Jo's school

4. Who moved into Billie Jo's school classroom?
    a. Mad Dog Craddock
    b. Arley Wanderdale
    c. A family
    d. A group of homeless children

5. Why did the children bring the fixings for soup to school?
    a. Because they had nothing better to do than cook
    b. Because Miss Freeland liked to teach cooking
    c. Because they fixed soup for needy children
    d. Because they shared with the family at lunch

6. What did they dress the new baby wear in *Birth*?
    a. A feed-sack nightgown that was Billie Jo's brother's
    b. A clean towel
    c. One of Billie Jo's robes
    d. A lovely outfit from the local department store

7. Which way did the family head when they left Billie Jo's school?
    a. North
    b. East
    c. South
    d. West

Dust Multiple Choice Quizzes continued page 18

8. What happened to the sugar that Sheriff Robertson found at the still on the Cimarron River?
    a. Sheriff Robertson poured it in the river.
    b. Sheriff Robertson gave a little bit to each family at the school.
    c. Sheriff Robertson gave it to Billie Jo's family
    d. Sheriff Robertson gave it to Miss Freeland to make sweet things for the children to eat.

9. Why is Billie Jo practicing piano again in *Dreams*?
    a. She is practicing because Mad Dog asked her to.
    b. She is practicing because Doc Rice suggested it.
    c. She is practicing for the contest being held at the Palace.
    d. She is practicing so that that she can play for Mad Dog.

10. What did Billie Jo win in the talent show competition at the Palace?
    a. She won a thousand dollars for first prize.
    b. She won third prize and one dollar.
    c. She won second prize and a handful of dimes.
    d. She won first prize and one hundred dollars.

Dust Multiple Choice Quizzes continued page 19

Section 10: *The Piano Player* through *Following in His Steps*

1. What does Billie Jo especially not want people to say when she plays the piano?
    a. "Billie Jo only plays to beat Mad Dog."
    b. "Billie Jo Kelby just plays to get a boy's attention."
    c. "Billie Jo Kelby plays like a cripple."
    d. "Billie Jo never did play as well as her mother."

2. What is "no good" in the poem of that name?
    a. The wheat
    b. The dust
    c. Billie Jo's piano playing
    d. Billie Jo's relationship with Mad Dog

3. What did Billie Jo have to check about the snow that fell in *Snow*?
    a. To see if it had any ice in it
    b. To see if it was wet enough to make a snowman
    c. To make sure it wasn't dust
    d. To make sure it wasn't just sleet

4. What does Billie Jo think is her father's reason for wanting to attend night school?
    a. To learn better English
    b. To learn how to raise wheat better
    c. To make some friends because he is lonely
    d. To spend time with the ladies there

5. Why does Calb Hardly miss Pete Guymon in *Dust Pneumonia*?
    a. Because Pete brought him candy every time he visited
    b. Because Pete used to joke with him and ask about the Wildcats
    c. Because he and Pete used to trade baseball cards
    d. Because Pete was the only person who ever came to visit him

6. After all of the trauma of the dust storm, what does Billie Jo do at the end of the poem of that name?
    a. She turns the plates and glasses upside down, crawls into bed, and sleeps.
    b. She asks her father if she can go and live with Aunt Ellis in Lubbock.
    c. She tells her father she can't stay there anymore.
    d. She sits and cries for hours.

Dust Multiple Choice Quizzes continued page 20

7. What is the "broken promise" in the poem of that name?
   a. The broken promise is that Mad Dog didn't come to visit as he promised.
   b. The broken promise is that Billie Jo's father started drinking again.
   c. The broken promise is that Billie Jo's mother died.
   d. The broken promise is that it rained a little everywhere but in Billie Jo's neighborhood.

8. Who could make Billie Jo less eager to leave home?
   a. Mad Dog
   b. Arley Wanderdale
   c. Her mother
   d. Her father

9. What happened to Haydon Parley Nye's widow?
   a. She died two months after Haydon did.
   b. Come to find out, she actually had poisoned Haydon.
   c. She left Oklahoma and went west.
   d. She killed herself.

Dust Multiple Choice Quizzes continued page 21

SPRING 1935
Section 11: *Heartsick* through *Blankets of Black*

1. Who is the boy Billie Jo thinks of in *Heartsick*?
    a. Arley Wanderdale
    b. Her little brother, Franklin
    c. One of the Black Mesa Boys
    d. Mad Dog Craddock

2. What marks does Billie Jo's father have on him in *Skin*?
    a. He has pock marks from boyhood acne.
    b. He has raised spots on his nose, cheek, and neck.
    c. He has splintered places from handling wood.
    d. He has freckled like Billie Jo.

3. Why does Billie Jo say that she should steer clear of Mad Dog Craddock?
    a. Because he isn't the marrying kind
    b. Because she's had enough of quiet men
    c. Because he already has a girlfriend
    d. Because he's too old for her

4. What subject do people not talk about to Billie Jo's face?
    a. Dust
    b. Fire
    c. Her mother
    d. Her mother's piano

5. What is in the letter that Aunt Ellis sent to Billie Jo's father?
    a. An apology for not coming soon enough to save the baby
    b. An invitation for Billie Jo and her father to come to visit her
    c. An invitation to Aunt Ellis' wedding
    d. An invitation for Billie Jo to come and live with her in Lubbock

6. Why can't Billie Jo remember the names of the migrant workers who have gone out to California?
    a. Because she has a poor memory
    b. Because the migrants seldom tell her their names in the first place
    c. Because there are too many of them
    d. Because a lot of them have names that are hard to pronounce

Dust Multiple Choice Quizzes continued page 22

7. Whose funeral did Billie Jo and her father set out for?
   a. Her mother's
   b. Mr. Hardly's
   c. Grandma Lucas'
   d. Pete Guymon's

8. What wouldn't start at the end of *Blankets of Black*?
   a. The fire
   b. The truck
   c. The tractor
   d. The lead car in the funeral procession

Dust Multiple Choice Quizzes continued page 23

Section 12: *The Visit* through *Old Bones*

1. What kind of job was Mad Dog hoping to get in Amarillo?
   a. Anything that was available
   b. Something with the power company
   c. A job in an ice cream factory
   d. A job singing on the radio

2. Who wound up in a kind of freak show in Ontario?
   a. The Dionne Quintuplets
   b. Mad Dog Craddock
   c. Haydon P. Nye
   d. Aunt Ellis

3. What does Billie Jo's father put on the shelf above the piano beside her mother's book of poetry and her aunt's invitation?
   a. The papers about his government loan
   b. A note Billie Jo wrote to him
   c. A picture of Billie Jo's mother
   d. A picture of Billie Jo as a baby

4. What did Miss Freeland do when Billie Jo played the piano at graduation?
   a. She clapped harder than anybody else.
   b. She stood and applauded.
   c. She waved at Billie Jo.
   d. She started to cry.

5. What started filling up when the rain poured down?
   a. All the streets in Joyce City
   b. All the gullies around the house
   c. Billie Jo's father's near-finished pond
   d. The big kitchen pan that Billie Jo had set outside.

6. What did Billie Jo's father do after it rained and he got the tractor started?
   a. He did a kind of dance.
   b. He thanked God.
   c. He drove the tractor out to the fields.
   d. He sang.

Dust Multiple Choice Quizzes continued page 24

7. Who is singing in his saddle since the rain came?
    a. Gene Autry
    b. Billie Jo's father
    c. Calb Hardly
    d. Joe De La Flor

8. Why can't Billie Jo work for the CCC?
    a. Because she isn't strong enough
    b. Because she is too young and the wrong sex
    c. Because her father won't let her
    d. Because she doesn't own a set of tools

9. What was everybody in town doing at the Joyce City Hardware and Furniture Company on a Sunday afternoon?
    a. Buying everything in the store at a special sale
    b. Listening to Mad Dog Craddock sing in Amarillo
    c. Listening to a speech by President Roosevelt
    d. Signing up to enter a talent show contest

10. What did Harley Madden find at the church one Sunday?
    a. A thousand dollars in cash
    b. A book of poetry that had been Billie Jo's mother's
    c. A baby
    d. A three-year-old boy

11. Where did Billie Jo find the dimes her mother had saved from the money she earned playing piano?
    a. In one of the two boxes in her closet
    b. In her mother's chest of drawers
    c. Behind the sugar in the kitchen cabinet
    d. In an envelope in the box of her baby brother's nighties

12. What does Billie Jo's father say when she proposes that they go to see the dinosaur site?
    a. "Not this week. I'm too busy."
    b. He didn't say anything. They just didn't go.
    c. "It's best to let the dead rest."
    d. "No way am I going to drive all that way to see dinosaurs."

Dust Multiple Choice Quizzes continued page 25

SUMMER 1935
Section 13: *The Dream* through *Met*

1. What does Billie Jo liken the piano to in *The Dream*?
    a. The dust all around her
    b. Her mother
    c. Her feelings for Mad Dog Craddock
    d. Her father's quiet

2. What is the major reason that Billie Jo decides to leave home?
    a. Missing her mother
    b. Her father
    c. Feeling lonesome after Livie moved
    d. Feeling guilty about the fire

3. What direction does Billie Jo travel in when she leaves home?
    a. East
    b. North
    c. South
    d. West

4. How does Billie Jo feel after two days on the train?
    a. Proud of herself for having the courage to leave home
    b. Lonesome for her father's companionship
    c. Stiff and sore
    d. Cold and afraid

5. What did the man on the train take when he left Billie Jo?
    a. Billie Jo's coat
    b. Nothing
    c. Billie Jo's remaining biscuits
    d. The dog that Billie Jo had found at the train yard

6. What did Billie Jo think she would do with the picture that the man on the train left behind?
    a. Tear it up
    b. Keep it to show to the police
    c. Mail it to the police in his hometown
    d. Send it to the man's family to let them know he was still alive.

Dust Multiple Choice Quizzes continued page 26

7. Who did Billie Jo call when she got off the train in Flagstaff, Arizona?
    a. Mad Dog Craddock
    b. Vera Wanderdale
    c. Livie Killian
    d. Mr. Hardly to contact her father

8. What did Billie Jo decide wasn't any better, just different?
    a. Arizona
    b. Getting away
    c. The food in California
    d. The landscape she saw in California

9. What did Billie Jo call her father when he met her at the train station?
    a. "Dad"
    b. "Pa"
    c. "Dada"
    d. "Daddy"

10. What does Billie Jo's father promise to do in *Met*?
    a. He promises to see Doc Rice about his skin problem.
    b. He promises to be a better father.
    c. He promises to talk more.
    d. He promises never to remarry.

Dust Multiple Choice Quizzes continued page 27

AUTUMN 1935
Section 14: *Cut It Deep* through *November Dust*

1. What does Doc Rice tell Billie Jo to do about her hands?
    a. Quit picking at them, put ointment on them, and use them
    b. Get them operated on in Amarillo
    c. Try not to move them at all for a while
    d. Try to move them a little every other day

2. What does Billie Jo's father do that is out of the ordinary when Louise comes to dinner?
    a. He dances with her and Billie Jo.
    b. He talks all night long.
    c. He cleans up after dinner.
    d. He helps to set the table.

3. What did Billie Jo do even though she didn't intend to?
    a. Got angry at Louise
    b. Played the piano for Louise
    c. Let Louise see a picture of her mother
    d. Liked Louise

4. What is the only thing Billie Jo hopes Louise doesn't do?
    a. Marry her father
    b. Crowd her out of her father's life
    c. Talk her father into sending her to live with Aunt Ellis in Lubbock
    d. Come around too often

5. In *Not Everywhere*, where does Billie Jo not want Louise to go with her and her father?
    a. To Amarillo to hear Mad Dog sing
    b. To dinner in Joyce City
    c. To visit her mother and the baby's grave
    d. To visit their secret place on the property

6. What does Billie Jo like best about Louise?
    a. The way Louise laughs
    b. The fact that Louise loves her father
    c. That Louise doesn't tell her what to do but just nods
    d. The way that Louise stays out of her business

Dust Multiple Choice Quizzes continued page 28

7. What is "holding its own" in *November Dust*?
   a. The pond that Billie Jo's father dug
   b. The wheat that Billie Jo's father planted in August
   c. The family's financial situation
   d. The relationship between Billie Jo and her father

8. What are the poppies doing in *Thanksgiving List*?
   a. Blooming in the mountains
   b. Dying off for the year
   c. Blooming on the grave of Billie Jo's mother and the baby
   d. Blooming right next to the pond

9. Why does Billie Jo think she is what she is?
   a. Because of her father
   b. Because of the dust
   c. Because of her mother
   d. Because of the piano

10. How did Louise and Billie Jo's father meet?
    a. At a bar in Guymon
    b. Louise was Billie Jo's father's night school teacher
    c. Louise took an English class with Billie Jo's father
    d. At church

11. How did Billie Jo's father let her mother know he intended to marry Louise?
    a. He laid a note on her grave.
    b. He thought about her a lot one day.
    c. He asked Billie Jo to tell her.
    d. He went to the gravesite and informed her of his intentions.

12. What was Louise's betrothal gift to Billie Jo's father?
    a. A thousand dollars
    b. Six bushels of wheat
    c. A second mule
    d. A new tractor

Answer Key: Multiple Choice Quizzes
Out of the Dust

Section 1	Section 2	Section 3	Section 4	Section 5	Section 6
1 D	1 B	1 A	1 C	1 B	1 C
2 C	2 B	2 A	2 A	2 C	2 D
3 C	3 C	3 B	3 B	3 B	3 C
4 A	4 D	4 C	4 B	4 B	4 D
5 B	5 C	5 D	5 D	5 B	5 C
6 A	6 A	6 C	6 B	6 B	6 B
7 C	7 C	7 D	7 C	7 C	7 A
8 A	8 B		8 C	8 C	8 B
			9 D	9 C	9 A
			10 D	10 C	10 D
			11 C	11 B	11 C
			12 C	12 C`	12 B

Section 7	Section 8	Section 9	Section 10	Section 11	Section 12
1 D	1 C	1 B	1 C	1 D	1 D
2 C	2 B	2 C	2 C	2 B	2 A
3 A	3 B	3 A	3 C	3 B	3 A
4 C	4 A	4 C	4 D	4 B	4 D
5 C	5 A	5 D	5 B	5 D	5 C
6 B	6 B	6 A	6 A	6 C	6 C
7 A	7 A	7 D	7 D	7 C	7 D
	8 B	8 D	8 C	8 B	8 B
	9 A	9 C	9 A		9 B
	10 C	10 B			10 C
					11 D
					12 C

Section 13	Section 14
1 B	1 A
2 B	2 C
3 D	3 D
4 C	4 B
5 C	5 C
6 D	6 C
7 D	7 A
8 B	8 C
9 D	9 B
10 A	10 B
	11 D
	12 C

VOCABULARY WORKSHEETS

Vocabulary
Out of the Dust

Section 1 Part I: Using Prior Knowledge and Contextual Clues
Below are the sentences in which the vocabulary words appear in the text. Read the sentence. Use any clues you can find in the sentence combined with your prior knowledge, and write what you think the words in bold mean.

1. Ma **crouched**,/barefoot, bare bottomed/over the swept boards,/because that's where Daddy said it'd be best.

2. I came too fast for the doctor,/**bawling** as soon as Daddy wiped his hand around/inside my mouth.

3. They pledged **revenge** on the rabbit population; wagering who could kill more.

4. They **scowl** as they pass on the street.

5. She always gets **testy** about my playing,/even though she's the one who truly taught me.

6. …but anyhow,/she was **distracted** enough,/I was determined enough,/this time I got just what I wanted.

Part II: Determining the Meaning: Match the vocabulary words to their dictionary definitions.

___ 1. crouched   A. sidetracked; diverted
___ 2. bawling   B. punishment in return for insult or injury
___ 3. revenge   C. irritable; touchy
___ 4. scowl   D. stooped
___ 5. testy   E. crying out loud
___ 6. distracted   F. frown

Dust Vocabulary continued page 2

Section 2 Part I: Using Prior Knowledge and Contextual Clues
Below are the sentences in which the vocabulary words appear in the text. Read the sentence. Use any clues you can find in the sentence combined with your prior knowledge, and write what you think the words in bold mean.

1. …and we're all **whittled** down to the bone these days…

2. I **squinted** back at him as I gave him Ma's order.

3. …and thinking about the secondhand music/in a **moldy** box at the shop in Joyce City…

4. We shake out our napkins,/spread them on our laps,/and flip over our glasses and plates,/**exposing** neat circles,/round comments/on what life would be without dust.

5. *Breaking **Drought***

Part II: Determining the Meaning: Match the vocabulary words to their dictionary definitions.

___ 7. whittled   A. revealing
___ 8. squinted   B. a long period of low rainfall
___ 9. moldy   C. reduced gradually
___10. exposing   D. musty or stale in odor or taste
___11. drought   E. looked at with eyes partly closed

Dust Vocabulary continued page 3

Section 3 Part I: Using Prior Knowledge and Contextual Clues
Below are the sentences in which the vocabulary words appear in the text. Read the sentence. Use any clues you can find in the sentence combined with your prior knowledge, and write what you think the words in bold mean.

1. …I remember being **dazzled** by her/whenever she played the piano.

2. …but sometimes I think she's/just plain **jealous**/when I'm at the piano/and she's not.

3. While Ma and Daddy slept/the dust came,/tearing up fields where the winter wheat,/set for **harvest** in June,/stood helpless.

4. The wind **snatched** that snow right off the fields…

Part II: Determining the Meaning: Match the vocabulary words to their dictionary definitions.

___ 12. dazzled   A.   envious
___ 13. jealous   B.   seized or grabbed
___ 14. harvest   C.   amazed or bewildered with spectacular display
___ 15. snatched   D.   gathering in of a crop

Dust Vocabulary continued page 4

Section 4 Part I: Using Prior Knowledge and Contextual Clues
Below are the sentences in which the vocabulary words appear in the text. Read the sentence. Use any clues you can find in the sentence combined with your prior knowledge, and write what you think the words in bold mean.

1. One quarter of the wheat is lost; blown away or **withered** up.

2. I **wince** at the sight of his rib-thin cattle.

3. To eat them now,/so **tart**,/would turn my mouth inside out,/would make my stomach groan.

4. On Sunday,/winds came,/bringing a red dust/like prairie fire,/hot and peppery,/**searing** the inside of my nose,/the whites of my eyes.

5. The **combines** gave started moving across the fields…

Part II: Determining the Meaning: Match the vocabulary words to their dictionary definitions.

___16. withered   A.   scorching or burning the surface of
___17. wince   B.   harvesting machines
___18. tart   C.   dried up; shriveled
___19. searing   D.   to shrink or start involuntarily, as in pain or distress
___20. combines   E.   having a sharp pungent taste; sour

Dust Vocabulary continued page 5

Section 5 Part I: Using Prior Knowledge and Contextual Clues
Below are the sentences in which the vocabulary words appear in the text. Read the sentence. Use any clues you can find in the sentence combined with your prior knowledge, and write what you think the words in bold mean.

1. *Dionne **Quintuplets***

2. Daddy/put a pail of **kerosene**/next to the stove….

3. I pushed her to the ground,/**desperate** to save her….

4. He bathed my burns in **antiseptic**.

5. Sand **chafed** inside my clothes,/against my skin.

6. It **whirred** like a thousand engines.

Part II: Determining the Meaning: Match the vocabulary words to their dictionary definitions.

___21. quintuplets   A. wore sore by rubbing
___22. kerosene   B. produced an airy vibrating sound
___23. desperate   C. one of five offspring born in a single birth
___24. antiseptic   D. a thin oil used as a fuel
___25. chafed   E. despairing; abandoning all hope
___26. whirred   F. destroyer of disease-carrying microorganisms

Dust Vocabulary continued page 6

Section 6 Part I: Using Prior Knowledge and Contextual Clues
Below are the sentences in which the vocabulary words appear in the text. Read the sentence. Use any clues you can find in the sentence combined with your prior knowledge, and write what you think the words in bold mean.

1. My father, **hunched** over, said nothing.

2. They didn't say a word about my father/drinking himself/into a **stupor**/while Ma writhed, begging for water.

3. My father stares out across his land,/empty but for a few withered stalks/like the **tufts** on an old man's head.

4. We squeezed more cattle,/more sheep,/onto less land,/and they grazed down the **stubble**/till they reached root.

Part II: Determining the Meaning: Match the vocabulary words to their dictionary definitions.

___27. hunched   A.   short stiff stalks that remain after harvesting
___28. stupor   B.   bent
___29. tufts   C.   short cluster of strands, as of hair or grass
___30. stubble   D.   a state of reduced sensibility; a daze

Dust Vocabulary continued page 7

Section 7 Part I: Using Prior Knowledge and Contextual Clues
Below are the sentences in which the vocabulary words appear in the text. Read the sentence. Use any clues you can find in the sentence combined with your prior knowledge, and write what you think the words in bold mean.

1. Vera Wanderdale/is putting on a dance **revue** at the Palace....

2. He doesn't stare at my **deformed** hands.

3. There were pictures of the **Panhandle** in the old days....

4. ...and a **sketch** of a little girl holding an enormous cat/in her lap.

Part II: Determining the Meaning: Match the vocabulary words to their dictionary definitions.

___31. revue   A. a hasty or undetailed drawing or painting
___32. deformed   B. narrow strip of land projecting from a larger area
___33. Panhandle   C. a musical show
___34. sketch   D. disfigured

Dust Vocabulary continued page 8

Section 8 Part I: Using Prior Knowledge and Contextual Clues
Below are the sentences in which the vocabulary words appear in the text. Read the sentence. Use any clues you can find in the sentence combined with your prior knowledge, and write what you think the words in bold mean.

1. Dust/piles up like snow/across the **prairie**….

2. …**dunes** leaning against fences,/mountains of dust pushing over barns.

3. He gathers **thistle** to feed what's left of his cattle,/his bone-thin cattle….

4. I place a wet cloth over my nose to keep/from breathing dust/and wipe the **grime** tracings from around my mouth,/and shiver, thinking of Ma.

5. …Mr. Kincannon hires my father/to pull his Olds out of the **muck** on Route 64.

6. My father stares at me/while I sit across from him at the table,/while I wash dishes in the basin,/my back to him,/the picked and **festered** bits of my hands in agony.

Part II: Determining the Meaning: Match the vocabulary words to their dictionary definitions.

___35. prairie   A.   a moist sticky mixture, especially of mud and filth
___36. dunes   B.   irritated; generating pus
___37. thistle   C.   large area of flat or rolling grassland
___38. grime   D.   hills or ridges of wind-blown sand (or dust)
___39. muck   E.   weedy plants with prickly leaves and purple flowers
___40. festered   F.   black dirt or soot clinging to a surface

Dust Vocabulary continued page 9

Section 9 Part I: Using Prior Knowledge and Contextual Clues
Below are the sentences in which the vocabulary words appear in the text. Read the sentence. Use any clues you can find in the sentence combined with your prior knowledge, and write what you think the words in bold mean.

1. …Out feet flying,/me and my father,/on the wooden floor **whirling**/to Arley Wanderdale and the Black Mesa Boys.

2. We share it at lunch with our guests,/the family of **migrants** who have moved out from dust/and Depression/and moved into our classroom.

3. The grandma takes care of the children,/bringing them out when the dust isn't blowing/letting them chase **tumbleweeds** across the field/behind the school….

4. Ashby and Rush were cooking up **moonshine**….

5. He found jugs of finished whiskey,/and barrels and barrels of **mash**….

6. Apple **pandowdy**!

7. I have practiced my best piece over and over/till my arms **throb**….

Part II: Determining the Meaning: Match the vocabulary words to their dictionary definitions.

___41. whirling   A. dish baked with sugar with thick top crust
___42. migrants   B. illegally distilled whiskey
___43. tumbleweed   C. pulsate; beat rapidly or violently
___44. moonshine   D. rotating rapidly; spinning
___45. mash   E. workers who travel around seeking work
___46. pandowdy   F. broken off plant that rolls around in the wind
___47. throb   G. mixture from which alcohol can be distilled

Dust Vocabulary continued page 10

Section 10 Part I: Using Prior Knowledge and Contextual Clues
Below are the sentences in which the vocabulary words appear in the text. Read the sentence. Use any clues you can find in the sentence combined with your prior knowledge, and write what you think the words in bold mean.

1. I don't say/it hurts like the **parched** earth with each note.

2. My father thought maybe/he ought to go to night school,/so if the farm failed/there'd be **prospects** to fall back on.

3. Calb Hardly teased Pete Guymon about his **wheezy**/truck sucking in dust.

4. ...the reassuring noises,/that no matter how **brittle** and sharp life seemed,/no matter how brittle and sharp she seemed, she was still my ma who loved me....

Part II: Determining the Meaning: Match the vocabulary words to their dictionary definitions.

___48. parched   A.   fragile; likely to break
___49. prospects   B.   making a hoarse whistling sound
___50. wheezy   C.   chances; possibilities
___51. brittle   D.   extremely dry; exposed to heat

Dust Vocabulary continued page 11

Section 11 Part I: Using Prior Knowledge and Contextual Clues
Below are the sentences in which the vocabulary words appear in the text. Read the sentence. Use any clues you can find in the sentence combined with your prior knowledge, and write what you think the words in bold mean.

1. The hard part is in spite of everything/if I had any boy **court** me,/it'd be Mad Dog Craddock.

2. My father and I,/we can't **soothe** each other.

3. Everything too ready to **ignite**.

4. So they separated the burning cars/and moved them down a **siding**,/away from any little thing that might catch if the flames hopped.

5. …until nothing remained but **warped** metal,/and twisted rails,/scorched dirt, and/charred ties.

6. One family came in/clutched together,/their pa, **divining** the path/with a long wooden rod.

Part II: Determining the Meaning: Match the vocabulary words to their dictionary definitions.

___52. court
___53. soothe
___54. ignite
___55 siding
___56. warped
___57. divining

A. calm; quiet; ease or relieve
B. catch fire
C. to seek affection of with intent to romance
D. bent; twisted
E. guessing
F. short section of railroad track

Dust Vocabulary continued page 12

Section 12 Part I: Using Prior Knowledge and Contextual Clues
Below are the sentences in which the vocabulary words appear in the text. Read the sentence. Use any clues you can find in the sentence combined with your prior knowledge, and write what you think the words in bold mean.

1. He just keep that invitation from her/**glowering** down at me from the shelf above the piano.

2. And then it changed,/halfway between snow and rain,/sleet,/**glazing** the earth.

3. Mrs. Love is taking applications/for boys to do **CCC** work.

4. …the **Lindberghs** said good night to one and lost it….

5. …a song for my little brother,/buried in Ma's arms on a **knoll** overlooking the/banks of the Beaver….

6. Bones/showing/in the green **shale**….

7. I think for a moment of Joe De La Flor/herding **brontosaurus** instead of   cattle/and I/smile.

Part II: Determining the Meaning: Match the vocabulary words to their dictionary definitions.

___58. glowering   A.   rock made of layers of sediment
___59. glazing   B.   Charles and Ann Lindbergh, whose baby was stolen
___60. CCC   C.   a small rounded hill
___61. Lindberghs   D.   large dinosaur of the Jurassic period
___62. knoll   E.   Civilian Conservation Corps
___63. shale   F.   looking or staring angrily or sullenly
___64. brontosaurus   G.   putting a thin glassy coating on

Dust Vocabulary continued page 13

Section 13 Part I: Using Prior Knowledge and Contextual Clues
Below are the sentences in which the vocabulary words appear in the text. Read the sentence. Use any clues you can find in the sentence combined with your prior knowledge, and write what you think the words in bold mean.

1. Now I slip under cover of darkness/inside a **boxcar**/and let the train carry me west.

2. I have seen the/camps of **dust-bowl** migrants/along the tracks.

3. I feed him two of the stale biscuits I've been **hoarding**/and save the rest.

4. The children in the picture were clean and serious,/looking out with a certain **longing**.

5. I tell him he is like the **sod**,/and I am like the wheat....

Part II: Determining the Meaning: Match the vocabulary words to their dictionary definitions.

___65. boxcar   A. grass-covered surface soil held together by roots
___65. dust-bowl   B. storing for future use
___67. hoarding   C. yearning or desire
___68. longing   D. fully enclosed railroad car used to carry freight
___69. sod   E. region reduced to aridity by drought and dust storms

Dust Vocabulary continued page 14

Section 14 Part I: Using Prior Knowledge and Contextual Clues
Below are the sentences in which the vocabulary words appear in the text. Read the sentence. Use any clues you can find in the sentence combined with your prior knowledge, and write what you think the words in bold mean.

1. Doc looks carefully at the **mottled** skin,/the stretched and striped and crackled skin.

2. Louise doesn't **flinch**. She looks straight back.

3. Prairie birds, the whistle of **gophers**, the wind/blowing,/the smell of grass/and spicy earth....

4. We are both confident, and a little **sassy**.

5. I was so full/my lids/sighed shut and Daddy walked with Louise instead of/me/out to Ma and Franklin's grave,/where he let Ma know his **intentions**.

6. Her **betrothal** gift to him.

Part II: Determining the Meaning: Match the vocabulary words to their dictionary definitions.

___70. mottled   A. engagement
___71. flinch   B. burrowing rodents
___72. gophers   C. impudent; brashly bold
___73. sassy   D. plans; goals
___74 intentions   E. recoil, as from something unpleasant
___75. betrothal   F. marked by spots or blotches

Answer Key: Vocabulary
Out of the Dust

1	D	26	B	51	C
2	E	27	B	52	A
3	B	28	D	53	B
4	F	29	C	54	F
5	C	30	A	55	D
6	A	31	C	56	E
7	C	32	D	57	F
8	E	33	B	58	G
9	D	34	A	59	E
10	A	35	C	60	B
11	B	36	D	61	C
12	C	37	E	62	A
13	A	38	F	63	D
14	D	39	A	64	D
15	B	40	B	65	E
16	C	41	A	66	B
17	D	42	E	67	C
18	E	43	F	68	A
19	A	44	B	69	F
20	B	45	G	70	E
21	C	46	A	71	B
22	D	47	D	72	C
23	E	48	C	73	D
24	F	49	B	74	A
25	A	50	A		

DAILY LESSONS

Lesson One

Objectives
1. To introduce the unit on **Out of the Dust**
2. To distribute books and other related materials
3. To begin consideration and discussion of one theme in **Out of the Dust**, namely having a dream

NOTE: Prior to this lesson, students should have been assigned to bring in some physical item (or a written physical description, photograph, or drawing of that item) that symbolizes a special dream of theirs. Borrowing from the story line in **Dust** in which Billie Jo Kelby has a special dream—namely to get out of the Oklahoma Dust Bowl--students should be encouraged to think about what dreams they would like to realize in their lifetime. You will have prepared ahead of time a bulletin board that has the title MY DREAM: THE THING I MOST WANT TO ACHIEVE. You may want to place pictures on the board. Remember to include pictures of both tangible and intangible things. For instance, you might have some valuable possessions pictured but will also want to show pictures of people embracing, people laughing together, people talking with doctors, etc. The point, of course, is that our most cherished dreams may be to achieve good health, to reach a deeper spiritual relationship, and to gain new friendships and strengthen old ones as to achieve a more tangible goal.

Activity #1
Ask students individually to explain the significance to them of their special dreams. If they can, they might explain how long they have had the dream, how they came to have it, what they think are their chances of achieving it, and when they think they might achieve it. After they have explained this, each student should go to the bulletin board and write a few words (using the infinitive "to") to describe their most cherished dream. If they have a picture representing their dream and there is space on the bulletin board, the students might post their pictures on the board as well. Students should be encouraged to keep all valuables with them and not leave them lying around in the classroom.

Activity #2
Distribute the materials students will use in this unit. Explain in detail how students are to use the materials.

Study Guides Students should read the study guide questions for each reading assignment before beginning the assignment to get a feeling for what events and ideas are important in the section they are about to read. After reading the section, students will (as a class or individually) answer the questions to review the important events and ideas from that section of the book. Students should keep the study guides as study materials for the unit test.

Lesson One continued page 2

<u>Vocabulary</u> As they are reading a section of the text, students will do vocabulary work related to the section they are reading. If they hunt for the vocabulary words as they read, students should be able to figure out the contextual meaning of the words. Following the completion of the reading of the book, there will be a vocabulary review of all the words used in the vocabulary assignments. Students should keep their vocabulary work as study materials for the unit test.
<u>A special note</u>: The words in this book are generally not very difficult. For some sections of the text, students will have little trouble matching up words with definitions. If you wish to make the vocabulary unit more challenging for your students, you might try having them use the words in sentences **not** relating to **Dust** and possibly trying to use all of the words in one section in a paragraph.

<u>Reading Assignment Sheet</u> You need to fill in the reading assignment sheet to let students know when their reading has to be completed. You can either write the assignment on a side black board or bulletin board and leave it there for students to see each day, or you can make copies for each student to have. In any case, advise students to become very familiar with the reading assignments so they know what is expected of them.

<u>Extra Activities Center</u> The Extra Activities Packet portion of this unit contains suggestions for a library of related books and articles in your classroom as well as crossword and word search puzzles. Make a center in your room where you will keep these materials for students to use. (Bring the books and articles in from the library and keep several copies of the puzzles on hand.) Explain to students that these materials are available for their use when they finish reading assignments or other class work early.

<u>Nonfiction Assignment Sheet</u> Explain to students that they each are to read at least one nonfiction piece from the in-class library at some time during the unit. Students will fill out a nonfiction assignment sheet after completing the reading to help you evaluate their reading experiences and to help the students to think about and evaluate their own reading.

<u>Books</u> Each school has its own rules and regulations regarding student use of school books. Advise students of the procedures that are usual for your school.

NONFICTION ASSIGNMENT SHEET
(To be completed after reading the required nonfiction article)

Name _____ Date _____ Class _____

Title of Nonfiction Read _____

Author _____ Publication Date _____

I. **Factual Summary**: Write a short summary of the piece you read.

II. **Vocabulary**:
   1. Which vocabulary words were difficult?

   2. What did you do to help yourself understand the words?

III. **Interpretation**: What was the main point the author wanted you to get from reading his or her work?

IV. **Criticism**:
   1. Which points of the piece did you agree with or find easy to believe? Why?

   2. Which points did you disagree with or find hard to believe? Why?

V. **Personal Response**:
   1. What do you think about this piece?

   2. How does this piece help you better understand the novel, **Out of the Dust**?

Oral Reading Evaluation
Out of the Dust

Name _____ Class _____ Date _____

SKILL	EXCELLENT	GOOD	AVERAGE	FAIR	POOR
Fluency	5	4	3	2	1
Clarity	5	4	3	2	1
Audibility	5	4	3	2	1
Pronunciation	5	4	3	2	1
_____	5	4	3	2	1
_____	5	4	3	2	1

Total _____ Grade _____

Comments:

Lesson Two

Objectives
1. To preview with study questions, do the vocabulary on, and read Section 1
2. To give students practice reading orally
3. To evaluate students' oral reading

Activity #1
Have students read Section 1 out loud in class. You probably know the best way to choose readers from your class: pick students at random, ask for volunteers, or use whatever other method works best for your group. If you have not yet completed an oral reading evaluation for your students this marking period, this would be a good opportunity to do so. A form is included with this unit for your convenience.

If students do not complete reading through Section 1 in class, they should do so prior to your next class meeting.

Lesson Three

Objective
To make students feel comfortable with the poetic format of the novel through a series of rewriting exercises.

Activity
This is a rewriting exercise in which students will rewrite the lines in some of the poems in order to become more familiar with the way they are constructed.

Some students will be put off by the fact that the story in **Out of the Dust** is told in blank verse poetry instead of the usual prose that they find in most novels. But deconstructing and reconstructing the poems' sentences will help them to feel more comfortable with the form of the novel.

Rewriting Exercise

Some students—indeed, some adults—will feel intimidated by a novel that is written in the form of over one hundred poems. This exercise is intended to give students a feeling of control over the contents of the poems and a better understanding of the various tones that can achieved through rewriting the contents of the poems. You may use the model poem, or you may move on to work with additional poems in the section. Your decision will be based on what you think your students can comfortably handle.

It doesn't really matter what you do with the poem. Just play with it so that your students feel comfortable with the poetic format because they have control over it.

Start with the poem, *Me and Mad Dog.* You might begin by having students deconstruct the poem and separate its individual sentences (and sentence fragments) and to put the information in the poem into numbered sentences, or you might want to ask students to put every thought into a separate sentence:

1. Arley Wanderdale, who teaches music once a week at our school, though Ma says he's no teacher at all, just a local song plugger, Arley asked if I'd like to play a piano solo at the Palace Theatre on Wednesday night. (Or, Arley Wanderdale teaches music once a week at our school. Ma says he's no teacher at all. She says he's a local song plugger. Arley asked if I'd like to play a piano solo at the Palace Theatre on Wednesday night.)

2. I grinned, pleased to be asked, and said, "That'd be all right." (Or, I grinned. I was pleased to be asked. I said, "That'd be all right.)

3. I didn't know if Ma would let me.

4. She's an old mule on the subject of my schooling.

5. She says, "You stay home on weeknights, Billie Jo."

6. And mostly that's what I do.

7. But Arley Wanderdale said, "The management asked me to bring them talent, Billie Jo, and I thought of you."

8. Even before Mad Dog Craddock? I wondered.

9. "You and Mad Dog," Arley Wanderdale said.

Rewriting Exercise continued page 2

10. Darn that blue-eyed boy with his fine face and his smooth voice, twice as good as a plowboy has any right to be. (Or, Darn that blue-eyed boy with his fine face and his smooth voice. He is twice as good as a plowboy has any right to be.)

11. I suspected Mad Dog had come first to Arley Wanderdale's mind, but I didn't get too riled.

12. Not so riled I couldn't say yes.

Then ask students to write all of the information in the poem in one paragraph containing nothing but complete sentences. There are any number of ways to do this:

> Arley Wanderdale, who teaches music once a week at our school (though Ma says he's really not a teacher at all, just a local song plugger), asked if I'd like to play a piano solo at the Palace Theatre on Wednesday night. I grinned, pleased to be asked, and said, "That'll be all right." I didn't know if Ma would let me. She's an old mule on the subject of my schooling. She says, "You stay home on weeknights, Billie Jo." And mostly that's what I do. But Arley Wanderdale said, "The management asked me to bring them talent, Billie Jo, and I thought of you." Even before Mad Dog Craddock? I wondered. "You and Mad Dog," Arley Wanderdale said. Darn that blue-eyed boy with his fine face and his smooth voice, I thought, twice as good as a plowboy has any right to be. I suspected Mad Dog had come first to Arley Wanderdale's mind, but I didn't get so riled that I couldn't say yes.

If you like, you can also have students write the paragraph in more formal prose. Then ask them how the message has changed along with the prose style:

> Arley Wanderdale, who teaches music once a week at our school, asked if I would like to play a piano solo at the Palace Theatre on Wednesday night. Ma says he is not really a teacher but is a song promoter. Still, I grinned, pleased to be asked, and said, "That would be all right." I didn't know if Ma would let me. She is very stubborn on the subject of my schooling. She says, "You stay home on weeknights, Billie Jo." And mostly that is what I do. But Arley Wanderdale said, "The management asked me to bring them talent, Billie Jo, and I thought of you." I wondered if Arley had thought of me even before Mad Dog Craddock. "You and Mad Dog," Arley Wanderdale said. Darn that blue-eyed boy with his fine face and his smooth voice, I thought, he is twice as good as a plowboy has any right to be. I suspected that Mad Dog had come first to Arley Wanderdale's mind, but I did not get so riled that I could not say yes.

Rewriting Exercise continued page 3

See if students can tell you how each the content changes when it is written in complete sentences and when it is written with some of the colloquialisms removed. Encourage them to think about why Karen Hesse wrote the novel in poetic form. What are the advantages of the poetic form? What are the advantages of the colloquialisms? Which version sounds most like a fourteen-year-old girl would sound? Does more formal language make the message of the poem more or less immediate? Do students respond to Billie Jo's message differently when her voice is changed?

You could also have students rewrite the poem using more modern colloquial terms: (Ma's a real pain on the subject of my schooling.) They could try to make it wordier and see what effect that would have: (My mother has always had very strong and profound feelings on the subject of my educational experiences.) They could try making it shorter and tighter and see what effect that would have: (Ma's strict about my schooling.)

Again, it doesn't make much difference, really, what you do with the poem. Just play with it and make the exercise fun for students. If time permits and you feel your students are capable of it, move on to other poems in the section. Give students choices of the types of rewrites they would like to do.

Lesson Four

<u>Objectives</u>
1. To preview with study questions, do the vocabulary on, and read Section 2.
2. To do some reading aloud in class to allow students to feel comfortable with the poems and to encourage them to see the different effects achieved with different readings
3. To allow students to do Section 3 preview work at home

<u>Activity #1</u>
Take time with the study questions and the vocabulary work so that you are sure that students are understanding the poems in Section 2. Break the class into small groups and have students work together to come up with the answers to the study questions and to do the vocabulary work.

<u>Activity #2</u>
Because none of the poems is very long, there is much opportunity here for reading aloud in class. Try getting different students to read parts of poems to see what different effects can be achieved by different readings. Assign some students to critique the student readings and tell how they feel the content changes as different students read the poems.

<u>Activity #3</u>
If you feel that your students are ready to move ahead and do some of the preview work at home, make the assignment that they do so. Collect the preview work for the first time or two that it is done at home, just to make sure that students understand what they are reading. If you have students do the preview work at home, you might like to give a Multiple Choice quiz the following class period or just pull two or three of the short answer questions out for class discussion.

Lesson Five

Objectives
1. To make sure the preview work has been done satisfactorily at home, or to do the preview work during class time
2. To read Section 3
3. To give students the opportunity to write from personal experience

Activity #1
Have students turn in the preview work if it was assigned for homework, or have students do the preview work in small groups or as a whole class during class time.

Activity #2
Read the third section of the text during class time. If you haven't already evaluated students on their oral reading abilities, now might be a good time to do so. Use the oral reading evaluation form, if you wish.

Activity #3
Give the students Writing Assignment #1 and allow them to write their papers during class time so that they have the opportunity to exchange papers with classmates prior to proofreading. If you run out of time, simply continue the writing assignment into the next class meeting.

Lesson Six

Objectives
1. To allow students to finish Writing Assignment #1 in class if time ran out in the preceding class
3. To test students' understanding of the first three sections of the novel
2. To preview with study questions, do the vocabulary on, and read Section 4

Activity #1
Give students as long as you deem is necessary for them to finish the first writing assignment during class time. Collect the assignment.

Activity #2
Use some of the questions from the Multiple Choice quizzes and test students' understanding of the three previous sections. After the quiz has been given, have students exchange papers and correct them right in the class. Collect the papers afterward, if you wish, but make sure that students have them to use for study purposes at the end of the unit.

Activity #3
Either as a whole class or in small groups, have students preview the fourth section of the novel with the study questions and the vocabulary worksheets. Then read Section 4 as a class. If you have choices to make about which poems you get to read in class, I suggest that you choose *Beat Wheat, Give Up on Wheat, What I Don't Know*, and *On the Road with Arley*.

Writing Assignment #1
Out of the Dust

PROMPT
In the sections of the novel that you have read so far, you have learned a lot about Billie Jo's life. You know something about several areas of her life: her birth, her parents, her community, her friends, her relationship with her mother, her passion (the piano), her value system, the kind of life she leads, her views in regard to her parents, her parents' relationship with each other, and her school life. In seventeen poems, then, the author of **Out of the Dust** has brought her heroine to life for you.

Your assignment is to choose one of two options:

One, you may write your assignment about yourself. Or, two, you may write your assignment about Billie Jo Kelby and why you would or would not like to have her as a close friend. If you choose the first option, you should be sure that at the end of your paper, your audience knows about at least three areas of your life. If you choose the second option, you should give at least three reasons for your decision.

Your choice should be relatively easy: if you find yourself interested in Billie Jo, positively or negatively, then write about her, or, if you are not particularly interested in Billie Jo but would like to write about your own life, then write about yourself.

PREWRITING
For whichever choice you have made, make a list of the things that you would like to talk about. If you are writing about your own life, make a list of what you consider to be important areas in your life. If you are writing about Billie Jo, make a list of what you consider to be favorable or unfavorable aspects of her life or traits that would make you want or not want her as a close friend.

Write down everything that occurs to you, and then go back and sort through them and combine ideas that are essentially the same. Pare your categories down until you have three basic points to make about yourself or about Billie Jo. Then you can begin to write your paper.

DRAFTING
You will probably want to begin your paper with an interesting introductory paragraph in which you state your main point: I would/would not want Billie Jo Kelby as a close friend. I lead an exciting life filled with interesting challenges. I lead a humdrum life filled with many boring experiences. Whatever you choose to say, state your point clearly in the first paragraph so that your audience knows what you are writing about.

Writing Assignment #1 continued page 2

Use your three main ideas for the body of the paper. Then write a conclusion that perhaps summarizes, looks to the future, or asks a question. Those are some of the ways that you can end your paper in a way that will be interesting to your audience.

PROMPT
When you finish the rough draft of your paper, ask a student who sits near you to read it. After reading your rough draft, he or she should tell you what he or she liked best about your work, which parts were difficult to understand, and ways in which your work could be improved. Reread your paper considering your critic's comments and make the corrections you think are necessary.

PROOFREADING
Do a final proofreading of your paper, double checking your grammar, spelling, organization, and the clarity of your ideas.

Lesson Seven

Objective
To explain the Nonfiction Reading Assignment to students and allow them time in the school library to get started on the assignment

Activity
Spend some time with the Nonfiction Reading Assignment Sheet (introduced earlier in this unit) and the topics and directions for the Nonfiction Reading Assignment that follow this lesson. Explain the assignment thoroughly to students, answer any questions that they may have, and then allow them to get underway on the assignment.

Notes to the teacher:

(1) There is nothing exhaustive or magical about my Nonfiction Reading Assignment list. If students have other ideas, their ideas may well be better choices for them. Also, if you would like to add to the list, by all means, do so. This is just a possible list to get you and your students started.

(2) You might want to alert the students to the fact that during the next class meeting you are going to ask them to tell one interesting fact that they have uncovered in their research for this assignment. Encourage students to be looking for something interesting that they think the rest of the class might like to know. Remind them that they are going to report <u>one interesting fact</u>, not give a report on their research. Giving this kind of very brief presentation will help students to discriminate items of particular interest from many different items and also to think clearly in terms of audience and how to choose information of interest to that audience.

Nonfiction Reading Assignment
Out of the Dust

For this assignment, you are to choose from the following list of topics some aspect of modern farming and research it. Be sure to choose something that is at least relatively interesting to you. If some topic not listed here appeals to you, you may talk with your teacher about researching it, but be sure that you have good reasons to justify why your topic is important and worth reading about.

If you and your teacher agree that it might be helpful, you may use the KWL form to get started on this assignment.

<u>Possible Topics:</u>

Wheat farming
Crop rotation
Amish farming
Dairy farming
Cattle farming
Pig farming
Bad health effects of farming
Responsible use of pesticides
Organic farming
Costs attached to farming
Family farms
Government subsidized farming
Animals on and around farms
Personality types of farmers
Spouses and families of farmers
Farm life
Seasonal pleasures
Seasonal difficulties
Why people farm
Why people leave farming
Country reliance on farmers
Soil considerations
County agents
Farm equipment and supplies
Learning to farm
Women farmers

KWL
Out of the Dust

Directions: Before reading, think about what you already know about your assigned topic. Write the information in the K column. Think about what you would like to find out from reading the book. Write your questions in the W column. After you have read the book, use the L column to write the answers to your questions from the W column and anything else you remember from the book.

K WHAT I KNOW	W WHAT I WANT TO FIND OUT	L WHAT I LEARNED

Lesson Eight

Objectives
1. To give students an opportunity to share something interesting from their Nonfiction Reading Assignment investigation with the rest of the class.
2. To do the preview and vocabulary work for and to read Section 5.

Activity #1
Just go around the room and have each student tell his or her topic and then tell his or her interesting fact. It might be helpful to have students stand as they give their interesting fact, if only to focus their thinking and get them to take this brief presentation seriously. If you like, you may choose in the early going those students who will most likely have their facts totally prepared. But with fair warning, every student should be able to come up with one interesting thing to tell classmates. This activity will give you another opportunity to observe students as they present information to the class.

Activity #2
Spend some time during class doing the preview work for and reading Section 5.
Note to the teacher: If you like, you may add more critical questions to the fact-based short answer questions for class discussion. For example, for this class period, you could start with the fact-based questions and vocabulary. Then, if your students are prepared to move on, you might ask some questions about the section of reading, such as, What kind of person would be able to go off and make his or her way at sixteen like the *Wild Boy of the Road*? Based on what you know already about Billie Jo's mother from earlier poems, how do you think she would have reacted if she had known Billie Jo was watching her in *Hope in a Drizzle*? What are the ironies in *The Accident*? Would there be any advantages in placing *A Tent of Pain* before *Nightmare*? Can the coming of the grasshoppers be viewed as a metaphor for the Kelby family's life?

There are no doubt many other questions such as these that would provide a good foundation for class discussion, but these are a start. You will know best what your students are capable of and how much background work you might have to do to get them ready for critical discussions.

Lesson Nine

Objectives
1.	To do the preview and vocabulary work for and to read Section 6
2.	To get students started on the class project

Activity #1
Spend some time doing the preview and vocabulary work for Section 6.
Note to the teacher: If you want to include some critical questions in your class discussion, you might want to consider the following: What are Billie Jo and her father actually seeing when she walks to town and when he stares out across his land in *Birthday*? How might Billie Jo's walk into town in *Birthday* differ from her walk into town in *Mr. Hardly's Money Handling*? In *Roots*, there is a failure on the part of government to understand the real needs of the people. Does that kind of failure still happen today? If not, why not? If so, can students give some examples of it? Have students look up the word **sod** and then explain why **sod** is a perfect metaphor for Billie Jo's father. In what way would a volcano like the one in *Kilauea* be a lot like a dust storm? In *Path of Our Sorrow*, does the author of **Out of the Dust** take the opportunity to offer a moralistic history lesson in the poem? Does that poem seem particularly effective to students or is it perhaps a little less effective than some of the others?

Activity #2
Give students time to get started on the class project if you are doing it. If not, you might give a multiple choice quiz or spend some additional time on critical questions.

Class Project
Project Modern Farming

Objectives

Through their reading of **Out of the Dust**, students should become at least a little bit intrigued by the subject of farming. If you teach in some regions of the country, farming may already be an integral part of your students' lives. In other regions, students may be hard pressed to make a connection between the food that appears in their grocery stores and the farmer tending crops.

In any event, this project will give students the opportunity to discover the educational components of their research, to relate their research to real life, and to take steps to improve a situation that they have investigated and found to be in need of improvement.

Students will be extracting from their Nonfiction Reading Assignment research an aspect of farming that could be improved through some sort of education. It may be that courses need to be offered on a subject at a local college or community center. It may be that information needs to be communicated to farmers via advertising of some sort. The people in the community may benefit from information about farming that can be conveyed in newspaper articles, television news reports, advertising, or letters to the editor. Perhaps some government programs need to be established to help certain types of farmers. Perhaps information needs to be conveyed to young people in the area about how to get started in farming, how to find a job on a farm for the summer, or how to plant and care for a garden on their own property.

Whatever the situation, students should be able to explain the educational need in a sentence or two and then proceed with the activities of the project.

THE PROJECT

This project is separate from the rest of the unit on **Out of the Dust**, so you can either use it while you are reading and reviewing the book or as a separate mini-unit after you have completed the unit test for **Dust**. Also, having it as a separate project enables you to either eliminate it or to use it, without disturbing the flow of the unit as a whole.

Activity #1

Explain the assignment fully to students. Set whatever time limits you wish to set for the project. If you do the project, I encourage you to allow some time(s) later in the unit for students to do updates on the work they are doing.

Project continued page 2

Activity #2
Try to find someone knowledgeable in your area who can interact with your class. This might be someone in a county extension office who could come and speak to your class. It might be a local farmer who would be willing to speak with students in the classroom. It might be a local farmer who would be willing to have students visit his or her farm one morning or afternoon. It could be someone who writes about farming for the local newspaper. And if you are unable to get someone to interact personally with your class, try at least to contact someone who is willing to respond to student letters or perhaps to make a tape about farming that the class can listen to.

Set up some kind of dialogue with the person or persons you choose. You might want to have students write questions and send them to the person. If you have found someone who will talk directly with the students, you can use the questions for the day that the person comes to class. If you like, you may have students write the letters inviting people to interact with the class, although you probably will save a lot of time by undertaking this responsibility yourself.

Activity #3
Have students choose one aspect of their Nonfiction Reading Assignment research that particularly interests them and that lends itself to educational improvement. It might be helpful to you to spend some time meeting very briefly with students before they get started on their project, just so that you are assured that they have chosen a workable topic. Students should be able to state their topic, tell in a sentence or two how they think education would help the situation they are working on, and then lay out at least two major ways in which they will work to improve the situation.

Activity #4
Have students actually get underway in making their educational improvements. You may allow class time for one or two days for this purpose or you may have the students do this work as homework.

Note to the teacher: Whatever educational steps students are going to take should actually be planned out. For example, if students think that a class should be offered at the local college, they should write up a course description, perhaps make up a mock syllabus, and include one or two items for the reading list. If they think that a letter writing campaign would be an educational improvement, then they should actually write some of the letters. If they think that an advertising campaign would be most beneficial, then they should actually design the advertising campaign. And so on.

Lesson Ten

Objectives
1. To do the preview and vocabulary work for and to read Section 7
2. To allow students the opportunity to write to inform.

Activity #1
Spend some time during class doing the preview and vocabulary work for and reading Section 7. Note to the teacher: If you want to include some critical discussion questions, ask students to look at *Mad Dog's Tale* and to consider the way the title and the way the poem is constructed. Encourage students to notice that the poem seems almost whimsical for the first nine lines and then its mood shifts radically with the line, *When I go home*.... Ask students to consider the effect on the reader of such a shift in mood. Have them look especially closely at the effectiveness of the last line and the way that it is separated from the rest of the poem. Then, if you want more questions, ask students if the uselessness of Billie Jo's hands in *Those Hands* is a metaphor for other aspects of her life. Consider also asking them what Billie Jo is really angry about in *Art Exhibit*.

Activity #2
Introduce the second writing assignment (Writing Assignment #2 - Writing to Inform). Make sure that students understand the assignment and then, if time allows, let them get started on the paper during class time.

Writing Assignment #2
Out of the Dust

PROMPT

In **Out of the Dust**, characters fill various roles and perform various tasks within those roles. For example, Billie Jo plays the piano, her mother manages a household and is wife and mother to Billie Jo and her father, Mr. Hardly runs a store, Pete Guymon delivers produce, and Miss Freeland teaches. Each of those people could write a paper on something that they do and could inform others how to do it.

Your assignment is to choose something that you do well and can explain fully. Don't panic if you think you don't have something interesting to write on. You may choose something as obviously interesting as playing a sport, performing on a musical instrument, singing in your church choir, or traveling to faraway locations. On the other hand, you could just as well choose something seemingly more mundane, such as setting the table for dinner, getting a younger brother or sister dressed to go out, babysitting a child or children, getting the house ready for company, convincing one or both of you parents to allow you to do something, or even getting from your house to school each morning.

Choose the activity that you would like to write about and then think about who would like to know the information. The person or people who would like to know the information is your audience.

PREWRITING

A good way to start is to think through the activity thoroughly. Make a list of the things involved in the activity. Don't leave out important steps just because they are obvious to you. If you are informing someone how to get from their house to yours, for example, it would not do to leave out a major right hand turn onto a specific street just because you are used to making the turn.

Then try to group the items on your list by type. If you can group them into three categories, you will be well on your way to being able to write a clear, thorough paper.

DRAFTING

Begin your paper with an introductory paragraph. Your first paragraph might contain, for example, the reason for your writing in the first place. Then use one paragraph in the body of the paper for each of your three categories. And, finally, write a concluding paragraph that sums up your previous points, asks a question, offers the possibility of further information if the reader wants it, or broadens the subject out just a bit to include additional uses for the information.

Writing Assignment #2 continued page 2

PROMPT
When you finish the rough draft of your paper, ask a student who sits near you to read it. After reading your rough draft, he or she should tell you what he or she liked best about your work, which parts were difficult to understand, and ways in which your work could be improved. Reread your paper considering your critic's comments and make the corrections you think are necessary.

PROOFREADING
Do a final proofreading of your paper, double checking your grammar, spelling, organization, and the clarity of your ideas.

Lesson Eleven

Objectives
1. To do the preview and vocabulary work for and to read Section 8
2. To test students' understanding of the sections of the novel read since the quiz in Lesson Six
3. To acquaint students with the use of metaphor in at least one of the poems in this section

Activity #1
Spend some time doing the preview and vocabulary work for Section 8, and then read the poems in the section.

Activity #2
Use some of the questions from the Multiple Choice quizzes and test students' understanding of Sections 4, 5, 6, 7, and 8. After the quiz has been given, have students exchange papers and correct them right in the class. Collect the papers afterward, if you wish, but make sure that students have them to use for study purposes at the end of the unit.

Activity #3
There are many ways to examine metaphors and similes in any piece of writing, but what I am encouraging you to do now is to spend some time discussing broader metaphor. For example, the dust in the novel is a metaphor for the bleakness and devastation of Billie Jo's life. Mrs. Brown's cereus plant is a metaphor for life in Oklahoma, able to bloom only out of reach of the brutal sun and wind.

Using the poem, *First Rain*, spend some time discussing metaphor. Encourage students to notice the way that the whole poem could be a metaphor for arriving at a symphonic performance, waiting for the symphony to warm up, hearing the first thrilling notes, hearing the whole symphony played, and then reveling in the resultant good feelings. Notice the number of verbs in the poem that could be musically translated with a little imagination: drumming, tapping, stroking, ponging, spilling, and gushing. Young students may better be able to translate these sounds and feelings to a rock concert than a symphonic one, but, really, any event for which one waits impatiently and then enjoys thoroughly will do.

Activity #4
If the activity on metaphor doesn't appeal to you, or if you think your students wouldn't benefit from it, try doing something different. Ask a big critical question such as, How well does the poetic form work in sections 6, 7, and 8 to get the author's ideas across? Would she have been better off just writing the novel in prose form? Would Billie Jo's voice change at all if the form of the book were changed?

Lesson Twelve

Objective
To give students an opportunity to understand the characters in **Out of the Dust** better by envisioning them in different contexts

Activity
Try to put aside one entire class to achieve this objective. What you are going to do is ask some of your students to do some role playing in front of the rest of the class. Because not everyone will have the opportunity to play a role in class, the other students will learn from observing. Both actors and observers should be encouraged to think about how the characters are going to act in each scenario. You will be the best judge of which students can be relied on to carry out the assignment with a reasonable degree of understanding and comfort.

Don't worry that you don't have enough time to accommodate this kind of role playing. Its object is not to rehearse or spend a lot of time preparing for the role playing. It is, instead, to think through very quickly how a character will act based on what students already know about them.

This activity will work best if you try to prepare the students to have a good time doing it. Make sure they realize that there is no totally right or totally wrong way to do the activity. Instead, they should listen closely to the scenarios that you lay out, think very quickly about how their assigned character would react to each, and then pretend to *be* that character to the best of their ability.

Choose the scenarios that you think your students will best understand. You may do one or two scenarios or all five. If you want, you can even make up new scenarios, with or without your students' help. Again, there is no right or wrong here. You are just moving the characters around a little bit in order to let students look at them a little differently and understand them a little bit better.

Read the scenario. Give students three to five minutes to prepare, and then give them five minutes to act out the scenario. The ONLY requirement is that students try as hard as possible to keep the character as he or she behaved in the book.

Scenario #1 Two students: Billie Jo Kelby and her teacher, Miss Freeland
Billie Jo has decided that she is definitely going to "run away from home." But first she wants to discuss her plans with her teacher, in which she has a great deal of faith and trust. So she sits down and tells Miss Freeland what is on her mind, how miserable she is, how much she misses her mother, how little her father understands her, and how much she wants to get away from her home. **Have Billie Jo share her thoughts and plans with Miss Freeland and then have Miss Freeland respond accordingly**

Character Exercise continued page 2

Scenario #2: Two students: Billie Jo and Mad Dog
Even though he is only sixteen and she is just fourteen, Mad Dog has decided that the best thing for him and for Billie Jo is for them to run away together. He believes that there are some regions of the country where they can be married without parental consent. Perhaps they could live in Amarillo, where he thinks he has a radio job lined up. Then, perhaps after a time, they can return to Oklahoma to live once more. ***Have Mad Dog propose his solution to Billie Jo's dilemmas and his itch to move on and then have Billie Jo respond to what he offers.***

Scenario #3: Two students: Billie Jo and her mother, who has returned to life temporarily
Billie Jo's mother has temporarily returned to life, and Billie Jo has an opportunity to talk with her and to share her thoughts about the accident, the death of the baby, and her life since her mother's death. Billie Jo has a lot that she wants to share, but, as always, she is having some difficulty talking to her mother. She knows that their time together is very limited. ***Have Billie Jo try to share her thoughts honestly with her mother and have her mother respond appropriately whenever it seems appropriate to do so.***

Scenario #4: Three students: Billie Jo, her father, and Aunt Ellis
Aunt Ellis has arrived at Billie Jo's home in Oklahoma demanding that Billie Jo come and live with her, at least for a while, in Lubbock. She feels that Billie Jo needs expert medical help for her hands, she wants to get Billie Jo a brand new piano to practice on, and she feels generally that Billie Jo's life will be much improved in Lubbock. She is talking with Billie Jo and her father together. ***Have Aunt Ellis state her views and then have Billie Jo and her father respond.***

Scenario #5: Three students: Arley and Vera Wanderdale and Mad Dog Craddock
Arley, Vera, and Mad Dog are talking together about Billie Jo. They are concerned about her and feel that she is sinking deeper into herself. They want very much to help her but don't really know how. ***Have Arley, Vera, and Mad Dog share a conversation about how to help Billie Jo.***

Lesson Thirteen

Objectives
1. To review the main events and ideas presented in **Out of the Dust** in the first eight sections
2. To do the preview and vocabulary work for and to read Section 9

Activity #1
Spend some time making sure that students are understanding the main events and ideas presented in the novel. You might want to allow students individually to state some aspects of Billie Jo's life that they have learned about so far, such as her birth, her parents, her friends, her community, her value system, the relationships between her parents, her goals in life, her desire to leave Oklahoma, her strength of character, etc. As they each state an aspect of Billie Jo's life that they have learned about, ask students to give an example of how they learned about that aspect in a poem. They need not know all of the names of the poems, but they should be able to describe the ideas and events in each well enough for everyone else in the class to recognize the poem.

Activity #2
Go over the preview and vocabulary work for Section 9 and then read that section in class.
Note to the teacher: If you want to include more critical thought discussion, you might ask students to contrast the two poems about President Roosevelt's birthday events: *Birthday for F.D.R.* and *The President's Ball*. Try to get students to focus on the differences in tone and mood between the two poems.

Lesson Fourteen

Objectives
1. To do the preview and vocabulary work for and to read Section 10
2. To give students the opportunity to update the rest of the class on their projects

Activity #1
Spend some time discussing the short answer questions and doing the vocabulary work for Section 10, then read Section 10 in class.

Note to the teacher: If you want to include some critical thought discussion in this class period, you might look at the poem, *Night School*, and discuss what the difference in audience impact would be had the author of the novel chosen to have Billie Jo express the feelings in that poem in prose form instead of poetry. She would have written something like, "I have mixed feelings about my father wanting to go to night school. He says he wants to learn some subject in case the farm fails, but, like my mother, I tell him that the farm won't fail. Secretly, though, I know that his real reason for wanting to go to night school is...." Compare that kind of recitation of Billie Jo's feelings with the poetic expression in *Night School*. Let students talk about which method they feel is more important to the purpose of accurately and feelingly conveying Billie Jo's emotions to an audience of readers.

Activity #2
Give students time to update the rest of the class on their projects. If time runs out, as it probably will, then carry this activity over into the next class period.

Lesson Fifteen

Objectives
1. To allow students time to complete their project updates
2. To do the preview and vocabulary work for and to read Section 11

Activity #1
Finish the project updates if you possibly can. It will help students to take the project seriously if they have the opportunity to talk about their work on it in class.

Activity #2
Spend some time answering the short answer questions and doing the vocabulary work for Section 11, then read the section in class.
Note to the teacher: If you want to include some critical thought questions in your discussion, you might spend some time with students talking about Billie Jo's increasing sense of life's people and events being out of her control and of life's somehow moving forward without her.

Notice how in *Heartsick*, for example, she is interested in Mad Dog Craddock but feels that he would never want her. She is restless and storms around the house but is unable to explain herself to her father. In *Skin*, she knows that her father needs to see a doctor but is unable to do more than to wonder about his situation. She recognizes in *Regrets* that she probably should avoid Mad Dog but cannot make herself do that. In *Fire on the Rails*, she acknowledges that people avoid mentioning fire to her but that they talk about her behind her back. She knows in *Mail Train* that her father is keeping the invitation letter from Aunt Ellis but she doesn't know why. The migrants in the poem of that name move past her faster and faster, going off to California in such numbers that she can't even remember their names. And in *Blankets of Black*, even a simple gesture like attending the funeral of someone in their community turns out badly for her and her father.

Try, if you can, to get students to think about how out of control Billie Jo's life seems to her. See if students can note some of the examples mentioned here as well as others that they can find in this section of poems.

Lesson Sixteen

Objectives
1. To do the preview and vocabulary work for Section 12 and to read that section in class
2. To test students' understanding of the sections of the novel covered since Lesson 11

Activity #1
Spend time discussing the short answer questions and doing the vocabulary work for Section 12, then read that section of the novel in class.

Activity #2
Choose some of the questions from the Multiple Choice Quizzes and test students' understanding of Sections 9, 10, 11, and 12 of the novel. After the students have marked the answers, ask them to exchange papers and correct them right in class. If you decide to collect the papers, be sure to return them to the students prior to the unit test so that they can use them for study purposes.

Lesson Seventeen

Objectives
1. To review the main ideas and events in the sections of the novel since Lesson 13
2. To do the preview and vocabulary work for Section 13 and to read that section in class

Activity #1
Spend some time reviewing the main ideas and events in Sections 9, 10, 11, and 12 of the novel. Be sure that students have the opportunity to ask questions if they have them.

Activity #2
Do the short answer discussion questions and vocabulary work for and read Section 13.

Note to the teacher: If you want to include some critical thought questions in your discussion, ask students to examine critically the poems *Midnight Truth* (in which Billie Jo decides to leave home), *Out of the Dust* (in which she actually slips onto a train and heads west), *Gone West* (in which she has been traveling in the boxcar for days), *Something Lost, Something Gained* (in which she has the opportunity to talk herself through everything that has happened to her, gains a better understanding of her life by talking with the man who shares the boxcar with her, and decides to return home), *Homeward Bound* (in which she summarizes her reason for going home), and *Met* (in which she comes to a sort of reconciliation with her "Daddy"). All of this transformation takes place rather quickly near the end of the novel. See if students found Billie Jo's leaving and returning compelling reading. Ask if they think that six poems is a long enough space to give to such a momentous experience in Billie Jo's life. In short, see how the change in Billie Jo strikes the students through the poems in this section.

Lesson Eighteen

<u>Objectives</u>
1.　To do the preview and vocabulary work for Section 14 and to read that section in class
2.　To give students the opportunity to write to persuade

<u>Activity #1</u>
Spend some time discussing the short answer questions and doing the vocabulary for Section 14 and then read that final section in class.

<u>Activity #2</u>
Explain Writing Assignment #3 (Writing to Persuade) to the students and allow them ample time to write their papers during class time, if at all possible. Directions for the assignment follow.

Writing Assignment #3
Out of the Dust

PROMPT
Now that you have finished reading the whole novel, **Out of the Dust**, you no doubt have an impression of whether the novel is a good book or not. Obviously, you, like everyone else, will have your own criteria for what makes a book good or not.

Your assignment is to write to an audience of students your own age who have not yet read the novel. Your goal is to convince them that **Out of the Dust** is or is not a good book for them to read.

PREWRITING
You should begin by establishing the criteria by which you will judge the novel. You may judge it, for example, on whether it was enjoyable to read, whether it is believable, whether it is educational, whether it is well written, or, indeed, by any other criteria you choose. Just be sure that you establish your criteria for judging the novel before you begin to write and that you stick with that criteria.

Whether you think positively or negatively about the book, make a list of all of the points you could consider to make your main point. Then try to put your points into categories. If possible, choose three categories.

DRAFTING
Write an introductory paragraph in which you tell what your criteria are and what main point you want to make in your paper. Then, in the body of the paper, explain the points in each of your categories thoroughly. And, finally, in your conclusion, end the paper by summarizing, by asking a question, or, perhaps, by suggesting a future course of action.

PROMPT
When you finish your rough draft of your paper, ask a student who sits near you to read it. In order to reflect the views of your audience, the student should try as hard as possible to pretend that he or she has not yet read the novel. After reading your rough draft, the other student should tell you what he or she liked best about your work, which parts were difficult to understand, and ways in which your work could be improved. Reread your paper considering your critic's comments and make the corrections you think are necessary.

PROOFREADING
Do a final proofreading of your paper, double checking your grammar, spelling, organization, and the clarity of your ideas.

Lesson Nineteen

Objectives
1.   To test students' knowledge of the whole novel, especially Sections 13 and 14
2.   To review the main ideas and events of the whole novel

Activity #1
Choose some questions from the Multiple Choice Quizzes to test students' knowledge of the novel. You may choose only questions from Sections 13 and 14, or you may combine a series of multiple choice quiz questions from all of the choices offered.

Activity #2
Spend some time making sure that students understand the main ideas and events of the whole novel. Answer any questions that students still have about the book.

Lesson Twenty

Objectives
1.   To have students exercise their critical thinking skills
2.   To try to relate some of the ideas in **Out of the Dust** to the students' lives

Activity #1
Choose the questions from the Extra Discussion Questions/Writing Assignments that seem most appropriate for your students. A class discussion of these questions is most effective if students have been given the opportunity to formulate answers to the questions prior to the discussion. To this end, you may either have all the students formulate answers to all of the questions, divide your class into groups and assign one or more questions to each group, or assign one question to each student in your class. The option you choose will obviously make a difference in the amount of class time needed for this activity.

Activity #2
After students have had ample time to formulate answers to the questions, begin your class discussion of the questions and the ideas presented by the questions. Be sure students take notes during the discussion so they have information to study for the unit test.

Activity #4
Try to spend some time on the critical/personal response and personal response questions in order to give the students ways to think personally about the book's events, main ideas, and characters.

Extra Discussion Questions/Writing Assignments
Out of the Dust

Interpretive
1. Which poem represents the climax of the novel? Explain your choice.

2. What is another possible title for the novel? Explain your choice.

3. What are the main conflicts in the novel, and how are they resolved?

4. What do you think are the three most important points that Karen Hesse tried to make in the book? Explain your choices.

5. How much time passes during the course of the novel? Do you think that the amount of time allows the author to adequately develop all of the characters in the novel?

6. Explain the role of Louise in the novel. What does she represent in the lives of Billie Jo and her father?

7. Give a complete character analysis of Billie Jo. Refer to specific examples from the text.

8. Give a complete character analysis of either Billie Jo's mother or her father. Refer to specific examples from the text.

Critical
9. Was there a point at which you thought that the novel would end on a totally downward note? A point at which you thought that Billie Jo might leave home and never return? A point at which you thought that her father might leave or die? If you always thought that the novel would end on a relatively upbeat note, why did you think that?

10. Explain the role of a character that never gets much development, like Mr. Hardly, Calb Hardly, Pete Guymon, Joe De La Flor, or Vera Wanderdale. How does the character help the novel's author to make the points she wants to make about Billie Jo and those closest to her?

11. Compare and contrast farming today with farming in the 1930's in Oklahoma.

12. Why did Billie Jo's mother have to die in the novel? Would the novel be substantially different if she had lived?

13. Explain a rationale for writing the novel in poetry form.

Extra Discussion Questions/Writing Assignments continued page 2

14. Other than Billie Jo, is there a main character of the novel? If so, who is it?

15. The novel is told from the standpoint of Billie Jo Kelby. In what way does that influence the reader's perception of her?

16. Look at the poems that have Mad Dog Craddock in them. Explain based on those poems what Billie Jo's relationship with Mad Dog is really like.

Critical/Personal Response

17. Is the novel believable? Why or why not?

18. If you were Billie Jo, what do you think you would have done after the death of the mother in the novel?

19. What or who is responsible for the discomfort suffered by the people in Oklahoma during the 1930's?

20. Who or what is responsible for the death of Billie Jo's mother in the novel?

21. **Out of the Dust** moves from Billie Jo's birth right into her current life. Would it have been helpful for the author to include more information about Billie Jo's earlier years? If so, what would have been added to the novel and to what purpose? If not, explain why not.

Personal Response

22. If you were living in very difficult circumstances and felt that you had no one to rely on, do you think you would have the strength to carry on?

23. What is the value of having parents who seem in control of their lives?

24. Suppose you had a friend who suffered a terrible disfiguring accident and lost his or her mother in the process, would you be able to help him or her? If so, how would you do it?

25. If you had a friend who felt guilty about his or her mother's death and had also suffered a great loss in a fire or some other calamity, would you be able to talk frankly to the friend about his or her feelings? Would you avoid the topic? What would you do?

Extra Discussion Questions/Writing Assignments continued page 3

<u>Quotations</u>: Think about the speaker of the quotation and its significance to the novel.

1. "They ought to just shut up./Betting on how many rabbits they can kill./Honestly!/Grown men clubbing bunnies to death./Makes me sick to my stomach."

2. "When I point my fingers at the keys,/the music/springs straight out of me."

3. "Chocolate milk for dinner, aren't we in clover!"

4. "I can turn the fields over,/start again./It's sure to rain soon./Wheat's sure to grow."

5. "…It's coming on spring, and he's a farmer."

6. "That's not your mama's way."

7. "Can't you see/what's happening, Bayard?/The wheat's not meant to be here."

8. "Look it, Pol, who's the farmer? You or me?"

9. "Most everyone's heard of *Madame Butterfly*."

10. "I only made it worse for Ma. She cried/for the pain of the water running into her sores,/she cried for the water that/would not soothe her throat/and quench her thirst/and the whole time/my father was in Guymon,/drinking."

11. "I knew you could."

12. "I guess he gets the sound out of him with the/songs he sings."

13. "I can't have my wife sleeping in the cold truck,/not now. Not with the baby coming so soon."

14. "Apple pandowdy!"

15. "I love this land,/no matter what."

16. "It's best to let the dead rest."

17. "My father's digging his own grave,/he calls it a pond,/but I know what he's up to."

Extra Discussion Questions/Writing Assignments continued page 4

18. "Getting away,/it wasn't any better./Just different./And lonely."

19. "We both stared in wonder/at the pond my daddy made/and she said,/a hole like that says a lot about a man."

20. "And the certainty of home, the one I live in,/and the one/that lives in me."

21. "And I know now that all the time I was trying to get/out of the dust,/the fact is,/what I am,/I am because of the dust./And what I am is good enough./Even for me."

Lesson Twenty-One

Objective
To complete discussions begun in Lesson Twenty

Activity
Since part of Lesson Twenty was taken up with giving students time to formulate answers, you will probably need a substantial portion of this class period to complete your class discussions.

Note to the teacher: If your discussions should finish early, you could give students the remainder of this class period to give updates on their projects or to ask any remaining questions they might have.

Lesson Twenty-Two

Objective
To review all of the vocabulary work done in this unit.

Activity
Choose one (or more) of the vocabulary review activities listed on the following pages and spend your class period as directed in the activity. Some of the materials for these review activities are located in the Extra Activities section in this unit.

Vocabulary Review Activities

1. Divide your class into two teams and have an old-fashioned spelling or definition bee.

2. Give each of your students (or students in groups of two, three, or four) a Vocabulary Word Search Puzzle based on **Out of the Dust**. The person or group to find all of the vocabulary words in the puzzle first wins.

3. Give students an **Out of the Dust** Vocabulary Word Search Puzzle without the word list. The person or group to find the most vocabulary words in the puzzle wins.

4. Use an **Out of the Dust** Vocabulary Crossword Puzzle. Put a puzzle onto a transparency on the overhead projector so everyone can see it and do the puzzle together as a class.

5. Give students an **Out of the Dust** Vocabulary Matching Worksheet to do.

6. Divide your class into two teams. Use the **Out of the Dust** vocabulary words with their letters jumbled as a word list. Student 1 from Team A faces off against Student 1 from Team B. You write the first jumbled word on the board. The first student (1A or 1B) to unscramble the word wins the chance for his or her team to score points. If 1A wins the jumble, go to student 2A and give him or her a definition. He or she must give you the correct spelling of the vocabulary word which fits that definition. If he or she does, Team A scores a point, and you give student 3A a definition for which you expect a correctly spelled matching vocabulary word. Continue giving Team A definitions until some team member makes an incorrect response. An incorrect response sends the game back to the jumbled-word face-off, this time with students 2A and 2B. Instead of repeating giving definitions to the first few students of each team, continue with the student after the one who gave the last incorrect response on the team. For example, if Team B wins the jumbled-word face-off and student 5B gave the last incorrect answer for Team B, you would start this round of definition questions with student 5B and so on. The team with the most points wins!

7. Have students write a story in which they correctly use as many vocabulary words as possible. Have students read their compositions orally. Post the most original compositions on your bulletin board.

Lesson Twenty-Three

Objective

To review the main ideas presented in **Out of the Dust** using the extra activities in the unit plan

Activity #1

Choose one of the review games/activities included in the Extra Activities Packet and spend your class period as outlined there.

Activity #2

Remind students that the Unit Test will be given during the next class meeting. Stress the review of the Study Guides and their class notes as a last-minute, brush-up review for homework.

Review Games/Activities - Out of the Dust

1. Ask the class to make up a unit test for **Out of the Dust** The test should have four sections: matching, short answer, multiple choice, and essay. Students may use half the period to make the test and then swap papers and use the other half of the class period to take a test a classmate has devised. The test should be taken open book. You may want to use the unit test included in this plan or take questions from the students' unit tests to formulate your own test.

2. Take half the period for students to make up short answer questions. Collect the questions. Divide the class into two teams. Alternate asking questions to individual members of teams A & B (like in a spelling bee). The question keeps going from A to B until it is correctly answered, then a new question is asked. A correct answer does not allow the team to get another question. Correct answers are +2 points; incorrect answers are -1 point.

3. Have students pair up and quiz each other from their study guides and class notes.

4. Give students an **Out of the Dust** crossword puzzle to complete.

5. Divide your class into two teams. Use the **Out of the Dust** crossword words with their letters jumbled as a word list. Student 1 from Team A faces off against Student 1 from Team B. You write the first jumbled word on the board. The first student (1A or 1B) to unscramble the word wins the chance for his or her team to score points. If 1A wins the jumble, go to student 2A and give him or her a clue. He or she must give you the correct word which matches that clue. If he or she does, Team A scores a point and you give student 3A a clue for which you expect another correct response. Continue giving Team A clues until some team member makes an incorrect response. An incorrect response sends the game back to the jumbled-word face-off, this time with students 2A and 2B. Instead of repeating giving clues to the first few students of each team, continue with the student after the one who gave the last incorrect response on the team. For example, if Team B wins the jumbled-word face-off and student 5B gave the last incorrect answer for Team B, you would start this round of clue questions with student 6B, and so on.

UNIT TESTS

Short Answer Unit Test #1
Out of the Dust

I. Matching/Identify

___ Mad Dog Craddock   A. woman Billie Jo's father is engaged to

___ Mr. Hardly   B. Billie Jo's father

___ Bayard Kelby   C. Billie Jo's romantic interest

___ Aunt Ellis   D. music promoter

___ Franklin   E. local grocer

___ Arley Wanderdale   F. has invited Billie Jo to live in Lubbock

___ Joe De La Flor   G. Billie Jo's little brother who died young

___ Louise   H. neighbor of the Kelby family

II. Short Answer

1. Why was the heroine of **Out of the Dust** named Billie Jo?

2. What does Billie Jo's father mean when he says, "The potatoes are peppered plenty tonight, Polly"?

3. Where does Billie Jo say that she would like to walk to one day like the boys who are leaving their homes?

4. What did Billie Jo do to make it worse for her mother while her father was in Guymon?

5. What does Billie Jo hear the women saying about her after her mother's death?

6. What does Billie Jo say she will never be able to forgive her father for as long as she lives?

Short Answer Unit Test #1 continued page 2

7. Who moved into Billie Jo's school classroom?

8. What does Billie Jo especially not want people to say when she plays the piano after the accident?

9. Who did Billie Jo call when she got off the train in Flagstaff, Arizona?

10. Why does Billie Jo think she is what she is?

III. Essay
Compare and contrast Billie Jo's mother and father, Polly and Bayard Kelby.

Short Answer Unit Test #1 continued page 3

IV. Vocabulary
Listen to the vocabulary word and spell it. After you have spelled all the words, go back and write down the definitions.

1.

2.

3.

4.

5.

6.

7.

8.

9.

10.

Key: Short Answer Unit Test #1
Out of the Dust

I. Matching/Identify

_C_ Mad Dog Craddock   A. woman Billie Jo's father is engaged to

_E_ Mr. Hardly   B. Billie Jo's father

_B_ Bayard Kelby   C. Billie Jo's romantic interest

_F_ Aunt Ellis   D. music promoter

_G_ Franklin   E. local grocer

_D_ Arley Wanderdale   F. has invited Billie Jo to live in Lubbock

_H_ Joe De La Flor   G. Billie Jo's little brother who died young

_A_ Louise   H. neighbor of the Kelby family

II. Short Answer

1. Why was the heroine of **Out of the Dust** named Billie Jo?
   She was named Billie Jo because her father wanted a boy.

2. What does Billie Jo's father mean when he says, "The potatoes are peppered plenty tonight, Polly"?
   He means that there is dust in the potatoes.

3. Where does Billie Jo say that she would like to walk to one day like the boys who are leaving their homes?
   She says she would like to walk her way West.

4. What did Billie Jo do to make it worse for her mother while her father was in Guymon?
   She tried to give her mother some water and spilled it on her because of her burned hands.

5. What does Billie Jo hear the women saying about her after her mother's death?
   She hears them saying, "Billie Jo threw the pail."

Key: Short Answer Unit Test #1 continued page 2

6. What does Billie Jo say she will never be able to forgive her father for as long as she lives?
She says she will never be able to forgive him for leaving the pail of kerosene near the stove.

7. Who moved into Billie Jo's school classroom?
A family moved into Billie Jo's school classroom.

8. What does Billie Jo especially not want people to say when she plays the piano after the accident?
She doesn't want them to say, "Billie Jo Kelby plays like a cripple."

9. Who did Billie Jo call when she got off the train in Flagstaff, Arizona?
She called Mr. Hardly to contact her father.

10. Why does Billie Jo think she is what she is?
She thinks she is what she is because of the dust.

III. Essay
Compare and contrast Billie Jo's mother and father, Polly and Bayard Kelby.

IV. Vocabulary
Choose ten of the vocabulary words to read orally for the vocabulary section of this test.

Short Answer Unit Test #2
Out of the Dust

I. Matching/Identify

___ Mad Dog Craddock   A. neighbor of the Kelby family

___ Mr. Hardly   B. Billie Jo's little brother who died young

___ Bayard Kelby   C. local grocer

___ Aunt Ellis   D. music promoter

___ Franklin   E. Billie Jo's romantic interest

___ Arley Wanderdale   F. has invited Billie Jo to live in Lubbock

___ Joe De La Flor   G. Billie Jo's father

___ Louise   H. woman Billie Jo's father is engaged to

II. Short Answer

1. What were the circumstances of Billie Jo's birth?

2. What does Billie Jo's mother say is the main reason that Billie Jo's father still believes in rain?

3. What did Billie Jo's mother say when told that Billie Jo scored at the top of the eighth grade at her school on an achievement test?

4. What is the major dispute between Billie Jo's mother and father in *Give Up on Wheat*?

5. What does Billie Jo's father say he remembers about World War I in France?

6. What was the initial cause of the accident that hurt Billie Jo and her mother?

7. What are the empty spaces that Billie Jo and her father are trying to fill?

Short Answer Unit Test #2 continued page 2

8. What did Billie Jo's mother do to "fit" Billie Jo's father?

9. What does Billie Jo think is her father's reason for wanting to attend night school?

10. What is the only thing Billie Jo hopes Louise doesn't do?

III. Quotations: Identify the speaker and explain the significance of these quotes:
1. "When I point my fingers at the keys,/the music/springs straight out of me."

2. "Chocolate milk for dinner, aren't we in clover!"

3. "I can turn the fields over,/start again./It's sure to rain soon./Wheat's sure to grow."

4. "…It's coming on spring, and he's a farmer."

5. "Can't you see/what's happening, Bayard?/The wheat's not meant to be here."

6. "I can't have my wife sleeping in the cold truck,/not now. Not with the baby coming so soon."

7. "Apple pandowdy!"

8. "My father's digging his own grave,/he calls it a pond,/but I know what he's up to."

9. "Getting away,/it wasn't any better./Just different./And lonely."

10. "We both stared in wonder/at the pond my daddy made/and she said,/a hole like that says a lot about a man."

Short Answer Unit Test #2 continued page 3

IV. Vocabulary
Listen to the vocabulary word and spell it. After you have spelled all the words, go back and write down the definitions.

1.

2.

3.

4.

5.

6.

7.

8.

9.

10.

Key: Short Answer Unit Test #2
Out of the Dust

I. Matching/Identify

_E_ Mad Dog Craddock   A. neighbor of the Kelby family

_C_ Mr. Hardly   B. Billie Jo's little brother who died young

_G_ Bayard Kelby   C. local grocer

_F_ Aunt Ellis   D. music promoter

_B_ Franklin   E. Billie Jo's romantic interest

_D_ Arley Wanderdale   F. has invited Billie Jo to live in Lubbock

_A_ Joe De La Flor   G. Billie Jo's father

_H_ Louise   H. woman Billie Jo's father is engaged to

II. Short Answer

1. What were the circumstances of Billie Jo's birth?
   Billie Jo was born at home on the kitchen floor.

2. What does Billie Jo's mother say is the main reason that Billie Jo's father still believes in rain?
   She says he still believes in rain because spring is coming on and he's a farmer.

3. What did Billie Jo's mother say when told that Billie Jo scored at the top of the eighth grade at her school on an achievement test?
   Her mother said, "I knew you could."

4. What is the major dispute between Billie Jo's mother and father in *Give Up on Wheat*?
   She thinks he should put in a pond or try some other crops, and he wants to stick with wheat.

5. What does Billie Jo's father say he remembers about World War I in France?
   Billie Jo's father remembers the poppies red on the graves of the dead.

6. What was the initial cause of the accident that hurt Billie Jo and her mother?
   The initial cause was that Billie Jo's father left a pail of kerosene sitting near the stove.

Key: Short Answer Unit Test #2 continued page 2

7. What are the empty spaces that Billie Jo and her father are trying to fill?
They are trying to fill the empty spaces left by Billie Jo's mother.

8. What did Billie Jo's mother do to "fit" Billie Jo's father?
She made herself over to fit him.

9. What does Billie Jo think is her father's reason for wanting to attend night school?
She thinks he wants to attend night school to spend time with the ladies there.

10. What is the only thing Billie Jo hopes Louise doesn't do?
She hopes that Louise doesn't crowd her out of her father's life.

III. Quotations: Identify the speaker and explain the significance of these quotes:

1. "When I point my fingers at the keys,/the music/springs straight out of me." (Billie Jo)

2. "Chocolate milk for dinner, aren't we in clover!" (Billie Jo's father)

3. "I can turn the fields over,/start again./It's sure to rain soon./Wheat's sure to grow." (Billie Jo's father)

4. "…It's coming on spring, and he's a farmer." (Billie Jo's mother)

5. "Can't you see/what's happening, Bayard?/The wheat's not meant to be here." (Billie Jo's mother)

6. "I can't have my wife sleeping in the cold truck,/not now. Not with the baby coming so soon." (The father of the family that moved into Billie Jo's school classroom)

7. "Apple pandowdy!" (Billie Jo)

8. "My father's digging his own grave,/he calls it a pond,/but I know what he's up to." (Billie Jo)

9. "Getting away,/it wasn't any better./Just different./And lonely." (Billie Jo)

10. "We both stared in wonder/at the pond my daddy made/and she said,/a hole like that says a lot about a man." (Billie Jo)

Advanced Short Answer Unit Test
Out of the Dust

I. Matching/Identify

___ Mad Dog Craddock   A. neighbor of the Kelby family

___ Mr. Hardly   B. Billie Jo's little brother who died young

___ Bayard Kelby   C. local grocer

___ Aunt Ellis   D. music promoter

___ Franklin   E. Billie Jo's romantic interest

___ Arley Wanderdale   F. has invited Billie Jo to live in Lubbock

___ Joe De La Flor   G. Billie Jo's father

___ Louise   H. woman Billie Jo's father is engaged to

II. Short Answer

1. Explain the role of a character that never gets much development, like Mr. Hardly, Calb Hardly, Pete Guymon, Joe De La Flor, or Vera Wanderdale. Choose one character and tell how the character helps the novel's author to make the points she wants to make about Billie Jo and those closest to her.

2. Explain a rationale for writing the novel in poetry form.

3. Why did Billie Jo's mother have to die in the novel? Would the novel be substantially different if she had lived?

Advanced Short Answer Unit Test continued page 2

4. Other than Billie Jo, is there a main character in the novel? If so, who is it?

5. The novel is told from the standpoint of Billie Jo Kelby. In what way does that influence the reader's perception of her?

III. Essay
Who or what is responsible for the death of Billie Jo's mother in the novel?

Advanced Short Answer Unit Test continued page 3

IV. Vocabulary
Listen to the vocabulary words and write them down. After you have written down all the words, write a paragraph in which you use all the words. The paragraph must in some way relate to **Out of the Dust**.

1.

2.

3.

4.

5.

6.

7.

8.

9.

10.

Paragraph

Multiple Choice-Matching Unit Test #1
Out of the Dust

I. Matching/Identify

___ Mad Dog Craddock   A. woman Billie Jo's father is engaged to

___ Mr. Hardly   B. Billie Jo's father

___ Bayard Kelby   C. Billie Jo's romantic interest

___ Aunt Ellis   D. music promoter

___ Franklin   E. local grocer

___ Arley Wanderdale   F. has invited Billie Jo to live in Lubbock

___ Joe De La Flor   G. Billie Jo's little brother who died young

___ Louise   H. neighbor of the Kelby family

II. Multiple Choice
1. Why was the heroine of **Out of the Dust** named Billie Jo?
    a. Because she looked like a country singer
    b. Because that was her grandmother's name
    c. Because her father wanted a boy
    d. Because that was the name of her mother's childhood friend

2. What does Billie Jo's father mean when he says, "The potatoes are peppered plenty tonight, Polly"?
    a. He means that Billie Jo's mother has spoiled the meal again.
    b. He means that she forgot to put pepper on the potatoes.
    c. He means that there is dust on the potatoes.
    d. He is just making a little joke between them.

3. Where does Billie Jo say that she would like to walk to one day like the boys who are leaving their homes?
    a. At least to Amarillo
    b. Her way West
    c. East to the White House
    d. All the way into Texas

Multiple Choice-Matching Unit Test #1 continued page 2

4. What did Billie Jo do to make it worse for her mother while her father was in Guymon?
   a. She wouldn't give her mother any water.
   b. She tried to give her mother some water and spilled it on her because of her burned hands.
   c. She touched her mother's burned body.
   d. She tried to turn her mother over to make her more comfortable.

5. What does Billie Jo hear the women saying about her after her mother's death?
   a. "Billie Jo just doesn't know any better."
   b. "Billie Jo should go and live with her Aunt Ellis."
   c. "Billie Jo has no feelings at all."
   d. "Billie Jo threw the pail."

6. What does Billie Jo say she will never be able to forgive her father for as long as she lives?
   a. Leaving the pail of kerosene near the stove
   b. Going off and drinking
   c. Not talking to her about her mother
   d. Not praising her

7. Who moved into Billie Jo's school classroom?
   a. Mad Dog Craddock
   b. Arley Wanderdale
   c. A family
   d. A group of homeless children

8. What does Billie Jo especially not want people to say when she plays the piano after the accident?
   a. "Billie Jo only plays to beat Mad Dog."
   b. "Billie Jo Kelby just plays to get a boy's attention."
   c. "Billie Jo Kelby plays like a cripple."
   d. "Billie Jo never did play as well as her mother."

9. Who did Billie Jo call when she got off the train in Flagstaff, Arizona?
   a. Mad Dog Craddock
   b. Vera Wanderdale
   c. Livie Killian
   d. Mr. Hardly to contact her father

Multiple Choice-Matching Unit Test #1 continued page 3

10. Why does Billie Jo think she is what she is?
    a. Because of her father
    b. Because of the dust
    c. Because of her mother
    d. Because of the piano

III. Quotations: Identify the speaker:
    A=Billie Jo   **B**=Billie Jo's mother
    C=Billie Jo's father **D**=The father of the family in the classroom

1. "When I point my fingers at the keys,/the music/springs straight out of me."

2. "Chocolate milk for dinner, aren't we in clover!"

3. "I can turn the fields over,/start again./It's sure to rain soon./Wheat's sure to grow."

4. "…It's coming on spring, and he's a farmer."

5. "Can't you see/what's happening, Bayard?/The wheat's not meant to be here."

6. "I can't have my wife sleeping in the cold truck,/not now. Not with the baby coming so soon."

7. "Apple pandowdy!"

8. "My father's digging his own grave,/he calls it a pond,/but I know what he's up to."

9. "Getting away,/it wasn't any better./Just different./And lonely."

10. "We both stared in wonder/at the pond my daddy made/and she said,/a hole like that says a lot about a man."

Multiple Choice-Matching Unit Test #1 continued page 4

IV. Vocabulary (Matching)

1.	crouched	A.	grassy surface soil held together by roots
2.	scowl	B.	engagement
3.	testy	C.	extremely dry; exposed to heat
4.	whittled	D.	narrow strip of land projecting from larger one
5.	drought	E.	a state of reduced sensibility; a daze
6.	harvest	F.	dried up; shriveled
7.	withered	G.	reduced gradually
8.	searing	H.	stooped
9.	desperate	I.	frown
10.	chafed	J.	irritable; touchy
11.	stupor	K.	a long period of low rainfall
12.	deformed	L.	gathering in of a crop
13.	Panhandle	M.	scorching or burning the surface of
14.	grime	N.	despairing; abandoning all hope
15.	muck	O.	wore sore by rubbing
16.	migrants	P.	disfigured
17.	parched	Q.	black dirt or soot clinging to a surface
18.	brittle	R.	moist sticky mixture, especially mud and filth
19.	sod	S.	workers who travel around seeking work
20.	betrothal	T.	fragile; likely to break

Multiple Choice-Matching Unit Test #2
Out of the Dust

I. Matching/Identify

___ Mad Dog Craddock   A. neighbor of the Kelby family

___ Mr. Hardly   B. Billie Jo's little brother who died young

___ Bayard Kelby   C. local grocer

___ Aunt Ellis   D. music promoter

___ Franklin   E. Billie Jo's romantic interest

___ Arley Wanderdale   F. has invited Billie Jo to live in Lubbock

___ Joe De La Flor   G. Billie Jo's father

___ Louise   H. woman Billie Jo's father is engaged to

II. Multiple Choice
1. What were the circumstances of Billie Jo's birth?
    a. She was born in the new hospital in Amarillo.
    b. She was born in a taxicab on the way to the hospital.
    c. She was born in the barn during a dust storm.
    d. She was born at home on the kitchen floor.

2. What does Billie Jo's mother say is the main reason that Billie Jo's father still believes in rain?
    a. Because he is foolish
    b. Because he is a Kelby
    c. Because spring is coming and he's a farmer
    d. Because he has no idea how to be a farmer

3. What did Billie Jo's mother say when told that Billie Jo scored at the top of the eighth grade at her school on an achievement test?
    a. "Very good, Billie Jo."
    b. "Great going, girl."
    c. "I knew you could."
    d. "I didn't think you had it in you."

4. What is the major dispute between Billie Jo's mother and father in *Give Up on Wheat*?
   a. She wants to move west, and he wants to stay put.
   b. She wants to raise sugar cane, and he wants to raise barley.
   c. She wants him to cut back on the wheat he grows.
   d. She thinks he should put in a pond or try some other crops, and he wants to stick with wheat.

5. What does Billie Jo's father say he remembers about World War I in France?
   a. All of the dead soldiers
   b. The great food offered by the French people
   c. The poppies red on the graves of the dead
   d. The great wine

6. What was the initial cause of the accident that hurt Billie Jo and her mother?
   a. The fire was too hot.
   b. Her father left a pail of kerosene sitting near the stove.
   c. The pot of water boiled over.
   d. Her mother turned the pail of kerosene over.

7. What are the empty spaces that Billie Jo and her father are trying to fill?
   a. The long gaps in their conversations
   b. The great difference in their ages
   c. The empty spaces left by Billie Jo's mother
   d. The bad feelings between them

8. What did Billie Jo's mother do to "fit" Billie Jo's father?
   a. She pretended to like farm life.
   b. She pretended to love him.
   c. She made herself over to fit him.
   d. She took a farm extension course.

9. What does Billie Jo think is her father's reason for wanting to attend night school?
   a. To learn better English
   b. To learn how to raise wheat better
   c. To make some friends because he is lonely
   d. To spend time with the ladies there

10. What is the only thing Billie Jo hopes Louise doesn't do?
    a. Marry her father
    b. Crowd her out of her father's life
    c. Talk her father into sending her to live with Aunt Ellis in Lubbock
    d. Come around too often

Multiple Choice-Matching Unit Test #2 continued page 3

III. Essay
Other than Billie Jo, who is the main character in the novel? Be specific and use examples from the text to support your answer.

Multiple Choice-Matching Unit Test #2 continued page 4

IV. Vocabulary (Matching)

1. testy — A. grassy surface soil held together by roots
2. scowl — B. stooped
3. crouched — C. extremely dry; exposed to heat
4. whittled — D. narrow strip of land projecting from larger one
5. drought — E. dried up; shriveled
6. harvest — F. a state of reduced sensibility; a daze
7. Panhandle — G. reduced gradually
8. searing — H. engagement
9. grime — I. scorching or burning the surface of
10. chafed — J. disfigured
11. stupor — K. a long period of low rainfall
12. deformed — L. gathering in of a crop
13. withered — M. frown
14. desperate — N. despairing; abandoning all hope
15. muck — O. wore sore by rubbing
16. migrants — P. irritable; touchy
17. parched — Q. black dirt or soot clinging to a surface
18. brittle — R. moist sticky mixture, especially mud and filth
19. sod — S. workers who travel around seeking work
20. betrothal — T. fragile; likely to break

Multiple Choice Answer Sheet

UNIT TEST #1

Matching	Short Answer	Quotations	Vocabulary	
1 __	1 __	1 __	1 __	11 __
2 __	2 __	2 __	2 __	12 __
3 __	3 __	3 __	3 __	13 __
4 __	4 __	4 __	4 __	14 __
5 __	5 __	5 __	5 __	15 __
6 __	6 __	6 __	6 __	16 __
7 __	7 __	7 __	7 __	17 __
8 __	8 __	8 __	8 __	18 __
	9 __	9 __	9 __	19 __
	10 __	10 __	10 __	20 __

UNIT TEST #2

Matching	Short Answer	Vocabulary	
1 __	1 __	1 __	11 __
2 __	2 __	2 __	12 __
3 __	3 __	3 __	13 __
4 __	4 __	4 __	14 __
5 __	5 __	5 __	15 __
6 __	6 __	6 __	16 __
7 __	7 __	7 __	17 __
8 __	8 __	8 __	18 __
	9 __	9 __	19 __
	10 __	10 __	20 __

Multiple Choice Answer Key

UNIT TEST #1

Matching	Short Answer	Quotations	Vocabulary	
1 C	1 C	1 A	1 H	11 E
2 E	2 C	2 C	2 I	12 P
3 B	3 B	3 C	3 J	13 D
4 F	4 B	4 B	4 G	14 Q
5 G	5 D	5 B	5 K	15 R
6 D	6 A	6 D	6 L	16 S
7 H	7 C	7 A	7 F	17 C
8 A	8 C	8 A	8 M	18 T
	9 D	9 A	9 N	19 A
	10 B	10 A	10 O	20 B

UNIT TEST #2

Matching	Short Answer	Vocabulary	
1 E	1 D	1 P	11 F
2 C	2 C	2 M	12 J
3 G	3 C	3 B	13 E
4 F	4 D	4 G	14 N
5 B	5 C	5 K	15 R
6 D	6 B	6 L	16 S
7 A	7 C	7 D	17 C
8 H	8 C	8 I	18 T
	9 D	9 Q	19 A
	10 B	10 O	20 H

UNIT RESOURCE MATERIALS

Bulletin Board Ideas
Out of the Dust

1. Have each student in the class choose a television or stage actor or actress to play each of six main characters (Billie Jo, her mother, her father, Mad Dog Craddock, Arley Wanderdale, and Miss Freeland). Ask each student to write the name of each character on the card and next to it write his or her acting choice very clearly and carefully and explain briefly on the card why they think their actor or actress would be a good choice to play that character. Have each student tell the information on his or her card. Then post all of the index cards on the bulletin board. If your class is large and your bulletin board small, consider rotating the cards.

2. Karen Hesse has written several other books. Have students look in the school library for her books and try to get a sense of which each is about. Put some brightly colored paper on the bulletin board and have students write the name of one Karen Hesse book and one interesting piece of information about it. Encourage students to read all of the information posted so that perhaps they might get interested in reading one of the books.

3. Make a kind of writing mural out of one bulletin board in your classroom. Invite students to use the board to express their personal feelings about **Out of the Dust**. Ask students to take a minute at the beginning or end of each class period to write something that expresses their thoughts that day about the book, its ideas, its character, or its author. Set some guidelines about appropriateness of comments and then let students write whatever they want.

4. Save a portion of a black board to use as a bulletin board for rotating comments. Start each day with a comment that might be made by one of the characters in **Out of the Dust**. Sign your comment with the name of one of the characters. Invite students to make comments about the one you put up and sign their comment with the name of one of the other three characters. Try to build up some suspense every day about what comment will appear from which character. None of the comments need be from the book, only in character for the person making it.

5. Make a bulletin board listing the vocabulary words for this unit. As you complete sections of the novel and discuss the vocabulary for each section, write the definitions on the bulletin board. Encourage students to look at the board often so that they learn the words easily.

6. With the permission of the student writers, post the best writing assignments done for this unit.

Bulletin Board Ideas continued page 2

7. If you have students who can draw, ask them to sketch a picture of one of the major characters or a scene from **Out of the Dust** and post it on the bulletin board.

8. Ask students to look through magazines and find pictures of people that look like their idea of any of the five characters in **Out of the Dust**. Get the students to post their pictures on the bulletin board labeled with the names of the characters the pictures make them think of. If you run short of material to cover one day, you could point to each picture on the bulletin board and see if there is consensus in the class about whether the pictures are like the characters or not. Even if the class disagrees with a particular association, that doesn't make the picture chosen wrong. It only means that a student has his or her own conception of what the character is like. Maybe that student will feel free to explain what he or she is thinking about the character. This might enlarge everyone's thoughts about the characters and the book.

Extra Activities
Out of the Dust

One of the difficulties in teaching a book is that not all students read at the same speed. One student who likes to read may take the book home and finish it in a day or two. Sometimes a few students finish the in-class assignments early. The problem, then, is finding suitable extra activities for students.

One useful thing to do is to keep a little library in the classroom. For this unit on **Out of the Dust**, you might check out from the school or local library other related books and articles about child/parent relationships, radiation, starting a new business, caring for the elderly, rabbits, science fairs, etc. If possible, also have on hand some copies of Karen Hesse's other works so that students can read something else by the author if they choose to do so.

Other things you may keep on hand are puzzles. There are some in this unit directly relating to **Out of the Dust**. Feel free to duplicate them for your students' use.

Some students may like to draw or paint. You might devise a contest or allow some extra-credit grade for students who draw characters or scenes from **Out of the Dust**. Note, too, that if the students do not want to keep their drawings, you may pick up some extra bulletin board materials this way. If you have a contest and you supply the prize (a CD, a copy of another work by Hesse, a copy of a book on a subject similar to that in **Out of the Dust**, for example), you could possibly make the drawing itself a non-refundable entry fee. Make sure you assure students that you will continue to place their name on the board with the drawing. This can assure a student that years into the future his or her drawing will still be in his or her old classroom.

The pages which follow contain games, puzzles, and worksheets. The keys, when appropriate, immediately follow the puzzle or worksheet. There are two main groups of activities: one group for the unit; that is, generally relating to the text of **Out of the Dust**, and another group of activities related strictly to the vocabulary words in **Out of the Dust**.

Directions for these games, puzzles, and worksheets are self-explanatory. The object here is to provide you with extra materials you may use in any way you choose.

More Activities
Out of the Dust

1. Have students choose to "be" any of the main characters. Ask them to keep a journal daily in which they write about what happens to them—but in the voice and character of their chosen character. Everything they write in theirjournal, even if they want to make comments about class to you, should be done in character.

2. Encourage students to act out a few scenes of **Out of the Dust**. It is easy to adapt even the individual poems to dramatic form. Ask students to pretend that **Out of the Dust** is being made into a play or a film. Students could rehearse a few scenes and present them to the rest of the class. If they become practiced at it, they could even present the scenes to other classes in your school.

3. Encourage students to write a poem for the book from the standpoint of a character other than Billie Jo. The people and events will be the same, but they will be seen through someone else's eyes. This kind of exercise will make students look at the details of the book differently than they did on a first reading.

4. Have students pretend to be Billie Jo, her mother, her father, or Louise and ask them to write letters to Karen Hesse. In the letters they should try to get Hesse to rewrite all or parts of the novel in order to significantly change their role in the book.

5. Let interested students "teach" a class one day. If the number of interested students is sufficient, you could allow the students to work together, make a clear plan, and actually teach a whole class. Feel free to share your daily lesson plans with the students as they prepare to teach.

6. Have students design a CD cover for a piece of music that they think Billie Jo, her mother, or Mad Dog Craddock might like to make. They should name the piece of music and then design the cover in whatever way they think is appropriate.

7. Make a bulletin board with telephone numbers students can call for advice in case they want additional information about the subjects presented in **Out of the Dust**. For instance, if students wanted information about farming, kerosene, parent/child relationships, the Oklahoma Dust Bowl, crop rotation, the railroad, migrant workers, recipes containing apples, an opera like *Madame Butterfly*, dinosaurs, night school, song promoters, or any other topics you think would interest them, they would be able to gain easy access to it. Students might want this information for purposes of class or even for real life situations.

More Activities continued page 2

8. Ask students to pretend that someone from outer space has been deposited into the middle of the action presented in **Out of the Dust**. The students could pretend to be the alien and write a letter back to their planet describing the new world that they are observing.

9. Have students assume that they have become friends with any one of the major characters (Billie Jo, her mother, her father, Mad Dog, Arley Wanderdale, Miss Freeland) in the novel. The students should write a paper or have a discussion regarding the type of gift they would like to give to their chosen character and why.

10. Have students discuss which television show they believe would be the favorite of each of the major characters in the book.

11. Students could consider whether they would like to be Polly or Bayard Kelby's son or daughter. Have them explain why or why not they believe either of the characters would be a good parent.

12. Students could create original costumes for one or two of the characters in **Out of the Dust**. A costume could actually be made and modeled or a few costume designs could be drawn and posted around the classroom.

WORD SEARCH - OUT OF THE DUST

Words are placed backwards, forward, diagonally, up and down. Words listed below are included in the maze. Circle the hidden vocabulary words in the maze.

```
F R E E L A N D R U S S I A N S C J H S
M R G H S Y I G E B M K H V A G R I A S
E G E J E X L G W U R P R C B U A M R V
J L F A T Q K Q O T Z I U T B Y N R D V
X A Z W K C N T P T P L C F Z M B N L P
C R T I K T A L O E C P K E F O E E Y C
H I H D R K R T P R N Z E L L N R B F H
R Z N V B E F F P F X O L W O Y R U C K
N O W H E A T S I L L E B G R U Y E A Q
P N M G Q R Y M E Y C N Y L F Z I R S W
N A V N Q L Y A S R E N L S E V E S S L
D Q S J E E B K R D R O L Z I V L C E J
L R K J L Y Y T Z D E I O L X V L J J C
F L X P B L X G C V U D P F C Q S C W F
C R A D D O C K S Z S W S L D H J M D H
```

ARIZONA	DIONNE	GUYMON	NOBLE	RICE
ARLEY	ELLIS	HARDLY	NYE	ROMNEY
BAYARD	ELZIRE	JIM	POLLY	RUSSIAN
BUTTERFLY	FLOR	KELBY	POND	VERA
CEREUS	FRANKLIN	LIVIE	POPPIES	WHEAT
CRADDOCK	FREAK	LOUISE	POWER	
CRANBERRY	FREELAND	LUCAS	REUBEN	

CROSSWORD - OUT OF THE DUST

CROSSWORD CLUES - OUT OF THE DUST

ACROSS
1. The music promoter, ___ Wanderdale
4. Billie Jo's father got a job with Wireless ___
7. Mad Dog's last name
11. last name of Haydon P., the old time Oklahoman
12. Billie Jo's Aunt ___
13. The opera Billie Jo didn't know: Madame ___
16. Arley's wife
17. The funeral of Grandma ___ was important to the Kelbys
19. The quintuplets were turned into a ___ show
20. Kind of plant that bloomed at midnight & died at dawn
22. Billie Jo's mother wanted her husband to dig a ___
25. Joe De La ___ was Billie Jo's neighbor
26. The produce deliverer was Pete ___
27. Billie Jo's mother, ___ Kelby
28. Billie Jo didn't know how to make ___ sauce

DOWN
2. Last name of the local doctor
3. Mr. ___ was the local grocer
5. The crop that Billie Jo's father tried to grow
6. Mr. ___ quarreled about killing rabbits
8. Billie Jo called home from Flagstaff,___
9. Last name of the Canadian quintuplets
10. Billie Jo's last name
11. Mr/ __ quarreled with Mr. Romney
13. Billie Jo's father's first name
14. Billie Jo's brother who died young
15. ___ Killian left home to make his own way
17. The Killian daughter Billie Jo was friends with
18. Type of thistle Joe De La Flor would feed cattle
19. Miss ___ was Billie Jo's teacher
21. First name of the quintuplets' mother
22. Growing on the graves of soldiers in France
23. Woman Billie Jo's father gets engaged to
24. Man cleaning up the Crystal Hotel; ___ Martin

CROSSWORD ANSWER KEY - OUT OF THE DUST

MATCHING QUIZ/WORKSHEET 1 - Out Of The Dust

___ 1. JIM   A. Woman Billie Jo's father got engaged to
___ 2. BUTTERFLY   B. Mr. ___ was the local grocer.
___ 3. RUSSIAN   C. First name of the quintuplets' mother
___ 4. LUCAS   D. Miss ___ was Billie Jo's teacher.
___ 5. NOBLE   E. Kind of plant that bloomed at midnight and died at dawn
___ 6. CRANBERRY   F. Billie Jo's mother: ___ Kelby
___ 7. POLLY   G. Arley's wife
___ 8. BAYARD   H. Joe De La ___ was Billie Jo's neighbor.
___ 9. LOUISE   I. What was growing on the graves of soldiers in France
___10. CRADDOCK   J. ___ Killian left home to make his own way
___11. WHEAT   K. Last name of the Canadian quintuplets
___12. NYE   L. Billie Jo's last name
___13. KELBY   M. Type of thistle Joe De La Flor would feed cattle
___14. HARDLY   N. The opera Billie Jo didn't know was Madame ___
___15. FLOR   O. Produce deliverer: Pete ___
___16. CEREUS   P. Billie Jo didn't know how to make ___ sauce.
___17. GUYMON   Q. The Killian daughter Billie Jo was friends with.
___18. ARLEY   R. Last name of Haydon who was an old-time Oklahoman
___19. VERA   S. The funeral of Grandma ___ was important to the Kelbys.
___20. ELZIRE   T. Mr. ___ quarreled with Mr. Romney.
___21. DIONNE   U. The crop Billie Jo's father tried to grow
___22. POPPIES   V. The man cleaning up the Crystal Hotel was ___ Martin.
___23. LIVIE   W. The music promoter: ___ Wanderdale
___24. REUBEN   X. Mad Dog's last name
___25. FREELAND   Y. Billie Jo's father's last name

KEY: MATCHING QUIZ/WORKSHEET 1 - Out Of The Dust

V - 1.	JIM	A. Woman Billie Jo's father got engaged to
N - 2.	BUTTERFLY	B. Mr. ___ was the local grocer.
M - 3.	RUSSIAN	C. First name of the quintuplets' mother
S - 4.	LUCAS	D. Miss ___ was Billie Jo's teacher.
T - 5.	NOBLE	E. Kind of plant that bloomed at midnight and died at dawn
P - 6.	CRANBERRY	F. Billie Jo's mother: ___ Kelby
F - 7.	POLLY	G. Arley's wife
Y - 8.	BAYARD	H. Joe De La ___ was Billie Jo's neighbor.
A - 9.	LOUISE	I. What was growing on the graves of soldiers in France
X -10.	CRADDOCK	J. ___ Killian left home to make his own way
U -11.	WHEAT	K. Last name of the Canadian quintuplets
R -12.	NYE	L. Billie Jo's last name
L -13.	KELBY	M. Type of thistle Joe De La Flor would feed cattle
B -14.	HARDLY	N. The opera Billie Jo didn't know was Madame ___
H -15.	FLOR	O. Produce deliverer: Pete ___
E -16.	CEREUS	P. Billie Jo didn't know how to make ___ sauce.
O -17.	GUYMON	Q. The Killian daughter Billie Jo was friends with.
W 18.	ARLEY	R. Last name of Haydon who was an old-time Oklahoman
G -19.	VERA	S. The funeral of Grandma ___ was important to the Kelbys.
C -20.	ELZIRE	T. Mr. ___ quarreled with Mr. Romney.
K -21.	DIONNE	U. The crop Billie Jo's father tried to grow
I - 22.	POPPIES	V. The man cleaning up the Crystal Hotel was ___ Martin.
Q -23.	LIVIE	W. The music promoter: ___ Wanderdale
J - 24.	REUBEN	X. Mad Dog's last name
D -25.	FREELAND	Y. Billie Jo's father's last name

MATCHING QUIZ/WORKSHEET 2 - Out Of The Dust

___ 1. RICE A. Last name of the local doctor

___ 2. CRANBERRY B. Billie Jo's Aunt ___

___ 3. GUYMON C. Joe De La ___ was Billie Jo's neighbor.

___ 4. BAYARD D. The funeral of Grandma ___ was important to the Kelbys.

___ 5. BUTTERFLY E. The music promoter: ___ Wanderdale

___ 6. LOUISE F. The crop Billie Jo's father tried to grow

___ 7. KELBY G. Miss ___ was Billie Jo's teacher.

___ 8. NOBLE H. Produce deliverer: Pete ___

___ 9. LUCAS I. Billie Jo's mother: ___ Kelby

___10. ELZIRE J. The opera Billie Jo didn't know was Madame ___

___11. POLLY K. Arley's wife

___12. ARLEY L. Kind of plant that bloomed at midnight and died at dawn

___13. ELLIE M. Billie Jo's mother wanted her husband to dig a ___.

___14. HARDLY N. Billie Jo didn't know how to make ___ sauce.

___15. FRANKLIN O. Mr. ___ quarreled about killing rabbits.

___16. POPPIES P. First name of the quintuplets' mother

___17. ROMNEY Q. Type of thistle Joe De La Flor would feed cattle

___18. FREELAND R. Billie Jo's brother who died young

___19. WHEAT S. Mr. ___ quarreled with Mr. Romney.

___20. CEREUS T. Billie Jo's father got a job with Wireless ___.

___21. POND U. Woman Billie Jo's father got engaged to

___22. RUSSIAN V. What was growing on the graves of soldiers in France

___23. VERA W. Mr. ___ was the local grocer.

___24. FLOR X. Billie Jo's last name

___25. POWER Y. Billie Jo's father's last name

KEY: MATCHING QUIZ/WORKSHEET 2 - Out Of The Dust

A - 1.	RICE	A. Last name of the local doctor
N - 2.	CRANBERRY	B. Billie Jo's Aunt ___
H - 3.	GUYMON	C. Joe De La ___ was Billie Jo's neighbor.
Y - 4.	BAYARD	D. The funeral of Grandma ___ was important to the Kelbys.
J - 5.	BUTTERFLY	E. The music promoter: ___ Wanderdale
U - 6.	LOUISE	F. The crop Billie Jo's father tried to grow
X - 7.	KELBY	G. Miss ___ was Billie Jo's teacher.
S - 8.	NOBLE	H. Produce deliverer: Pete ___
D - 9.	LUCAS	I. Billie Jo's mother: ___ Kelby
P - 10.	ELZIRE	J. The opera Billie Jo didn't know was Madame ___
I - 11.	POLLY	K. Arley's wife
E - 12.	ARLEY	L. Kind of plant that bloomed at midnight and died at dawn
B - 13.	ELLIE	M. Billie Jo's mother wanted her husband to dig a ___.
W - 14.	HARDLY	N. Billie Jo didn't know how to make ___ sauce.
R - 15.	FRANKLIN	O. Mr. ___ quarreled about killing rabbits.
V - 16.	POPPIES	P. First name of the quintuplets' mother
O - 17.	ROMNEY	Q. Type of thistle Joe De La Flor would feed cattle
G - 18.	FREELAND	R. Billie Jo's brother who died young
F - 19.	WHEAT	S. Mr. ___ quarreled with Mr. Romney.
L - 20.	CEREUS	T. Billie Jo's father got a job with Wireless ___.
M - 21.	POND	U. Woman Billie Jo's father got engaged to
Q - 22.	RUSSIAN	V. What was growing on the graves of soldiers in France
K - 23.	VERA	W. Mr. ___ was the local grocer.
C - 24.	FLOR	X. Billie Jo's last name
T - 25.	POWER	Y. Billie Jo's father's last name

JUGGLE LETTER REVIEW GAME - OUT OF THE DUST

YLPOL	POLLY	Billie Jo's mother, _____ Kelby
DARYBA	BAYARD	Billie Jo's father's first name
BYKEL	KELBY	Billie Jo's last name
KRIFANNL	FRANKLIN	Billie Jo's brother who died young
LESLI	ELLIS	Billie Jo's Aunt _____
EYLAR	ARLEY	The music promoter, ___ Wanderdale
RAVE	VERA	Arley's wife
LDACPDRC	CRADDOCK	Mad Dog's last name
OYREMN	ROMNEY	Mr. ___ quarreled about killing rabbits
BENOL	NOBLE	Mr. ___ quarreled with Mr. Romney
VEILI	LIVIE	The Killian daughter Billie Jo was friends with
BEENUR	REUBEN	___ Killian left home to make his own way
RHYLDA	HARDLY	Mr. ___ was the local grocer
CIRE	RICE	Last name of the local doctor
ALEFNEDR	FREELAND	Miss ____ was Billie Jo's teacher
NONDIE	DIONNE	Last name of the Canadian quintuplets
RIZEEL	ELZIRE	First name of the quintuplets' mother
RLBUYTFET	BUTTERFLY	The opera Billie Jo didn't know was Madame ___
SEPIPOP	POPPIES	What was growing on the graves of soldiers in France
LFRO	FLOR	Joe De La ___ was Billie Jo's neighbor
HAWTE	WHEAT	The crop that Billie Jo's father tried to grow
DOPN	POND	Billie Jo's mother wanted her husband to dig a ____
SOULIE	LOUISE	Woman Billie Jo's father gets engaged to
SURECE	CEREUS	Kind of plant that bloomed at midnight and died at dawn
WOPER	POWER	Billie Jo's father got a job with Wireless ____
NRERRCYBA	CRANBERRY	Billie Jo didn't know how to make ____ sauce
MIJ	JIM	The man cleaning up the Crystal Hotel was ___ Martin
NURASIS	RUSSIAN	Type of thistle Joe De La Flor would feed cattle
NYUMGO	GUYMON	The produce deliverer was Pete ____
YEN	NYE	Last name of Haydon P. who was an old time Oklahoman
SACUL	LUCAS	The funeral of Grandma ___ was important to the Kelbys
RKAEF	FREAK	The quintuplets were turned into a _____ show
ROZINAA	ARIZONA	Billie Jo called home from Flagstaff, ____

VOCABULARY RESOURCES

VOCABULARY WORD SEARCH - OUT OF THE DUST

Words are placed backwards, forward, diagonally, up and down. Words listed below are included in the maze. Circle the hidden vocabulary words in the maze.

```
S K E T C H R L G C S C W H I R R E D Y
O O R U C U E I N R L T M H E F C E E T
D A O F C N V N I T I X U V I N N L F M
T V I T G C E D S H K M U B I R Y T A O
C V N S H H N B O R N E E W B S L S H L
D Y T Z X E G E P O O D F C S L H I C D
G U E W B D E R X B L R E A O H E H N Y
O G N I Z A L G E D L W S S C U T T D G
P P T E G Y H H W U A Y H N P S R E E M
H A I H S R M S A S D Z I E E E R T R O
E R O S T U P O R T M L Z V E E R L E T
R C N J H Y P Q P B F U R L T Z W A H T
S H S F G A N K E O R A C S E O Y P T L
T E S T Y T L J D W H V E K C D X S I E
V D E F O R M E D L V F Z S F R J D W D
```

CCC	FLINCH	MOLDY	SOD	WHEEZY
CHAFED	GLAZING	MOTTLED	SOOTHE	WHIRLING
COURT	GOPHERS	MUCK	STUBBLE	WHIRRED
DAZZLED	GRIME	PARCHED	STUPOR	WINCE
DEFORMED	HARVEST	REVENGE	TART	WITHERED
DESPERATE	HUNCHED	REVUE	TESTY	
DUNES	INTENTIONS	SASSY	THISTLE	
DUSTBOWL	KNOLL	SCOWL	THROB	
EXPOSING	LINDBERGHS	SHALE	TUFTS	
FESTERED	MASH	SKETCH	WARPED	

VOCABULARY CROSSWORD - OUT OF THE DUST

VOCABULARY CROSSWORD CLUES - OUT OF THE DUST

ACROSS
1. Grass covered surface soil held together by roots
3. Envious
9. Stooped
12. Dish baked with sugar with thick top crust
14. A musical show
16. Weedy plants with prickly leaves and purple flowers
20. Hills or ridges of wind-blown sand or dust
23. Short, stiff stalks that remain after harvesting
25. A long period of low rainfall
28. Civilian Conservation Corps
29. A moist, sticky mixture, especially of mud & filth
31. Small, rounded hill
32. Bent
33. Short section of railroad track
34. Dried up; shriveled

DOWN
1. Looked at with eyes partly closed
2. Despairing; abandoning all hope
4. Revealing
5. Charles and Ann, whose baby was stolen
6. Frown
7. Musty or stale in odor or taste
8. Punishment in return for insult or injury
10. Harvesting machines
11. Seized or grabbed
13. Irritable; touchy
15. Scorching or burning the surface of
17. Catch fire
18. Having a sharp pungent taste
19. Sidetracked; diverted
21. A thin oil used as a fuel
22. Short cluster of strands, as of hair or grass
24. Crying out loud
25. Amazed or bewildered with spectacular display
26. Black dirt or soot clinging to a surface
27. Mixture from which alcohol can be distilled
30. To seek affection of with intent to romance

VOCABULARY CROSSWORD ANSWER KEY - OUT OF THE DUST

S	O	D			J	E	A	L	O	U	S		M				R	
Q		E				X		I				C	R	O	U	C	H	E	D
U		S		S		P		N				O		L			O		V
I		P	A	N	D	O	W	D	Y			W		D		M		E
N		E		A		S		B			L		Y		B		N
T		R		T		U		E				T			I		G
E		A		C		R		R	E	V	U	E			N		E
D		T		H		E		G				S			E		S
		E		E				H				T	H	I	S	T	L	E
	D			D	U	N	E	S		K		Y		G		A		A
	I		T							E				N		R		R
	S	T	U	B	B	L	E			R				I		T		I
	T		F		A		D	R	O	U	G	H	T				N
	R		T		W		A		S		R		E				G
	A		S		L		Z		E		I				M	
C	C	C			I		Z		N		M	U	C	K		A	
	T			K	N	O	L	L		E			E		O		S
	E			G			E					H	U	N	C	H	E	S
	D				S	I	D	I	N	G		R				
											W	I	T	H	E	R	E	D

VOCABULARY WORKSHEET 1 - Out Of The Dust

___ 1. PARCHED A. Black dirt or soot clinging to a surface
___ 2. FLINCH B. Large area of flat or rolling grassland
___ 3. EXPOSING C. Revealing
___ 4. BOXCAR D. Destroyer of disease-carrying microorganisms
___ 5. REVENGE E. Recoil, as from something unpleasant
___ 6. SQUINTED F. Extremely dry; exposed to heat
___ 7. TESTY G. Despairing; abandoning all hope
___ 8. TUFTS H. Disfigured
___ 9. CROUCHED I. Making a hoarse whistling sound
___10. DIVINING J. Fully enclosed railroad car used to carry freight
___11. ANTISEPTIC K. Guessing
___12. GRIME L. Envious
___13. HOARDING M. Reduced gradually
___14. DESPERATE N. Short cluster of strands, as of hair or grass
___15. SCOWL O. Pulsate; beat rapidly or violently
___16. WARPED P. Punishment in return for insult or injury
___17. JEALOUS Q. Seized or grabbed
___18. SNATCHED R. Storing for future use
___19. BRITTLE S. Fragile; likely to break
___20. WHEEZY T. Rock made of layers of sediment
___21. WHITTLED U. Looked at with eyes partly closed
___22. PRAIRIE V. Irritable; touchy
___23. SHALE W. Stooped
___24. DEFORMED X. Bent; twisted
___25. THROB Y. Frown

KEY: VOCABULARY WORKSHEET 1 - Out Of The Dust

F - 1. PARCHED		A. Black dirt or soot clinging to a surface
E - 2. FLINCH		B. Large area of flat or rolling grassland
C - 3. EXPOSING		C. Revealing
J - 4. BOXCAR		D. Destroyer of disease-carrying microorganisms
P - 5. REVENGE		E. Recoil, as from something unpleasant
U - 6. SQUINTED		F. Extremely dry; exposed to heat
V - 7. TESTY		G. Despairing; abandoning all hope
N - 8. TUFTS		H. Disfigured
W - 9. CROUCHED		I. Making a hoarse whistling sound
K - 10. DIVINING		J. Fully enclosed railroad car used to carry freight
D - 11. ANTISEPTIC		K. Guessing
A - 12. GRIME		L. Envious
R - 13. HOARDING		M. Reduced gradually
G - 14. DESPERATE		N. Short cluster of strands, as of hair or grass
Y - 15. SCOWL		O. Pulsate; beat rapidly or violently
X - 16. WARPED		P. Punishment in return for insult or injury
L - 17. JEALOUS		Q. Seized or grabbed
Q - 18. SNATCHED		R. Storing for future use
S - 19. BRITTLE		S. Fragile; likely to break
I - 20. WHEEZY		T. Rock made of layers of sediment
M - 21. WHITTLED		U. Looked at with eyes partly closed
B - 22. PRAIRIE		V. Irritable; touchy
T - 23. SHALE		W. Stooped
H - 24. DEFORMED		X. Bent; twisted
O - 25. THROB		Y. Frown

VOCABULARY WORKSHEET 2 - Out Of The Dust

1. MIGRANTS — A. Illegally distilled whiskey
2. JEALOUS — B. Yearning or desire
3. DAZZLED — C. Sour
4. ANTISEPTIC — D. Catch fire
5. SASSY — E. Pulsate; beat rapidly or violently
6. REVENGE — F. Envious
7. WITHERED — G. Large area of flat or rolling grassland
8. PANDOWDY — H. Fragile; likely to break
9. BOXCAR — I. Dried up; shriveled
10. DESPERATE — J. Amazed or bewildered with spectacular display
11. PROSPECTS — K. Despairing; abandoning all hope
12. IGNITE — L. Short section of railroad track
13. WHIRLING — M. Marked by spots or blotches
14. STUBBLE — N. Destroyer of disease-carrying microorganisms
15. SOOTHE — O. Impudent; brashly bold
16. TART — P. Chances; possibilities
17. SHALE — Q. Short, stiff stalks that remain after harvesting
18. MOONSHINE — R. Fully enclosed railroad car used to carry freight
19. LONGING — S. Dish baked with sugar with thick top crust
20. SIDING — T. Irritable; touchy
21. BRITTLE — U. Calm; quiet; ease or relieve
22. TESTY — V. Rock made of layers of sediment
23. THROB — W. Punishment in return for insult or injury
24. PRAIRIE — X. Workers who travel around seeking work
25. MOTTLED — Y. Rotating rapidly; spinning

KEY: VOCABULARY WORKSHEET 1 - Out Of The Dust

X - 1.	MIGRANTS	A. Illegally distilled whiskey
F - 2.	JEALOUS	B. Yearning or desire
J - 3.	DAZZLED	C. Sour
N - 4.	ANTISEPTIC	D. Catch fire
O - 5.	SASSY	E. Pulsate; beat rapidly or violently
W - 6.	REVENGE	F. Envious
I - 7.	WITHERED	G. Large area of flat or rolling grassland
S - 8.	PANDOWDY	H. Fragile; likely to break
R - 9.	BOXCAR	I. Dried up; shriveled
K - 10.	DESPERATE	J. Amazed or bewildered with spectacular display
P - 11.	PROSPECTS	K. Despairing; abandoning all hope
D - 12.	IGNITE	L. Short section of railroad track
Y - 13.	WHIRLING	M. Marked by spots or blotches
Q - 14.	STUBBLE	N. Destroyer of disease-carrying microorganisms
U - 15.	SOOTHE	O. Impudent; brashly bold
C - 16.	TART	P. Chances; possibilities
V - 17.	SHALE	Q. Short, stiff stalks that remain after harvesting
A - 18.	MOONSHINE	R. Fully enclosed railroad car used to carry freight
B - 19.	LONGING	S. Dish baked with sugar with thick top crust
L - 20.	SIDING	T. Irritable; touchy
H - 21.	BRITTLE	U. Calm; quiet; ease or relieve
T - 22.	TESTY	V. Rock made of layers of sediment
E - 23.	THROB	W. Punishment in return for insult or injury
G - 24.	PRAIRIE	X. Workers who travel around seeking work
M - 25.	MOTTLED	Y. Rotating rapidly; spinning

VOCABULARY JUGGLE LETTER REVIEW GAME
OUT OF THE DUST

CDRUHOCE	CROUCHED	Stooped
GWANBLI	BAWLING	Crying out loud
NEGEERV	REVENGE	Punishment in return for insult or injury
SWLOC	SCOWL	Frown
YESTT	TESTY	Irritable; touchy
DCARDSECITT	DISTRACTED	Sidetracked; diverted
HELTIWDT	WHITTLED	Reduced gradually
TUSNEIQD	SQUINTED	Looked at with eyes partly closed
YLMOD	MOLDY	Musty or stale in odor or taste
SGXOEPNI	EXPOSING	Revealing
RUTHOGD	DROUGHT	A long period of low rainfall
ZALDEZD	DAZZLED	Amazed or bewildered with spectacular display
LAJSEUO	JEALOUS	Envious
ARTESVH	HARVEST	Gathering in of a crop
NDETASHC	SNATCHED	Seized or grabbed
RWIDHTEE	WITHERED	Dried up; shriveled
WCEIN	WINCE	To shrink or start involuntarily, as in pain or distress
RTTA	TART	Having a sharp pungent taste; sour
GRAENIS	SEARING	Scorching or burning the surface of
BEOCSNMI	COMBINES	Harvesting machines
TNQPUUTEIL	QUINTUPLET	One of five offspring born in a single birth
RNEEOKSE	KEROSENE	A thin oil used as a fuel
PRTEASEED	DESPERATE	Despairing; abandoning all hope
CIPTEISTNA	ANTISEPTIC	Destroyer of disease-carrying microorganisms
HADCEF	CHAFED	Wore sore by rubbing
REHDIWR	WHIRRED	Produced an airy vibrating sound
UEHDHCN	HUNCHED	Bent
OTSPRU	STUPOR	A state of reduced sensibility; a daze
SUTTF	TUFTS	Short cluster of strands, as of hair or grass
BLETBSU	STUBBLE	Short, stiff stalks that remain after harvesting
VEERU	REVUE	A musical show
DEEDMOFR	DEFORMED	Disfigured
ALENADPNH	PANHANDLE	Narrow strip of land projecting from a larger area
SHETCK	SKETCH	A hasty or undetailed drawing or painting
IRPIEAR	PRAIRIE	Large area of flat or rolling grassland
DESNU	DUNES	Hills or ridges of wind-blown sand (or dust)
HLTETSI	THISTLE	Weedy plants with prickly leaves and purple flowers
MRIEG	GRIME	Black dirt or soot clinging to a surface
KMCU	MUCK	A moist sticky mixture, especially of mud and filth
EEDRFTES	FESTERED	Irritated; generating pus

GLIWNHRI	WHIRLING	Rotating rapidly; spinning
TSAGIMNR	MIGRANTS	Workers who travel around seeking work
WUBEETDELM	TUMBLEWEED	Broken off plant that rolls around in the wind
SOMONENIH	MOONSHINE	Illegally distilled whiskey
SHAM	MASH	Mixture from which alcohol can be distilled
WYNAPOOD	PANDOWDY	Dish baked with sugar with thick top crust
BROTH	THROB	Pulsate; beat rapidly or violently
DHRACPE	PARCHED	Extremely dry; exposed to heat
OPPCETRSS	PROSPECTS	Chances; possibilities
ZHEWYE	WHEEZY	Making a hoarse whistling sound
IRTBELT	BRITTLE	Fragile; likely to break
TROUC	COURT	To seek affection of with intent to romance
HOTOES	SOOTHE	Calm; quiet; ease or relieve
TEIING	IGNITE	Catch fire
NIGSDI	SIDING	Short section of railroad track
RAWDEP	WARPED	Bent; twisted
GINNIVID	DIVINING	Guessing
GILEWGNOR	GLOWERING	Looking or staring angrily or sullenly
ILZGGNA	GLAZING	Putting a thing glassy coating on
BRSHLGEDIN	LINDBERGHS	Charles and Ann, whose baby was stolen
LONKL	KNOLL	Small rounded hill
ELHSA	SHALE	Rock made of layers of sediment
ROXACB	BOXCAR	Fully enclosed railroad car used to carry freight
TWUBDOLS	DUSTBOWL	Region reduced to aridity by drought and dust storms
RADHGONI	HOARDING	Storing for future use
NOGGLNI	LONGING	Yearning or desire
DOS	SOD	Grass-covered surface soil held together by roots
TOMDELT	MOTTLED	Marked by spots or blotches
HILFCN	FLINCH	Recoil, as from something unpleasant
SOGERPH	GOPHERS	Burrowing rodents
YSSSA	SASSY	Impudent; brashly bold
TTONNSNIE I	INTENTIONS	Plans; goals
BLARHOTTE	BETROTHAL	Engagement

www.ingramcontent.com/pod-product-compliance
Lightning Source LLC
Chambersburg PA
CBHW051407070526
44584CB00023B/3330